PRAISE FOR *THE GREAT NORTH ROAD*

*"I was going to ride the Great North Road and write about it...
but in the light of this annoyingly good book, I won't."*

Tim Moore

*"Weaving the history of the old road with the colour and the
characters of today, Steve proves that any journey is an adventure
if you know where to look."*

Alastair Humphreys

*"An enjoyable ode to a road that cyclists planning a trip will love,
with entertaining nuggets of trivia and history for anyone who
has ever hit the A1 for a long drive. Silk is a man on a mission,
snaking alongside the main carriages on his winding passage by
bike north via many a cafe and old coaching inn (many of which
Charles Dickens visited, apparently). This journey may just give
the lockdown Lycra brigade ideas."*

Tom Chesshyre

*"I love this book. I love the idea of considering something as
mundane and utilitarian as the A1(M) in a fascinating, historical
context. Who knew that behind this seemingly endless snake of
concrete and tarmac lies the makings of a fabulous journey of
pilgrimage? It is a joy to learn about the background to Steve's
journey and to follow him as he makes his way along his very
own Great North Road."*

Rachel Ann Cullen

THE GREAT NORTH ROAD

An Hachette UK Company
www.hachette.co.uk

Summersdale Publishers Ltd
Part of Octopus Publishing Group Limited
Carmelite House
50 Victoria Embankment
LONDON
EC4Y 0DZ
UK

www.summersdale.com

Printed and bound by CPI Group (UK) Ltd, Croydon, CR0 4YY

ISBN: 978-1-80007-049-3

THE GREAT NORTH ROAD

LONDON <u>TO</u> EDINBURGH
11 DAYS, 2 WHEELS AND 1 ANCIENT HIGHWAY

STEVE SILK

summersdale

CONTENTS

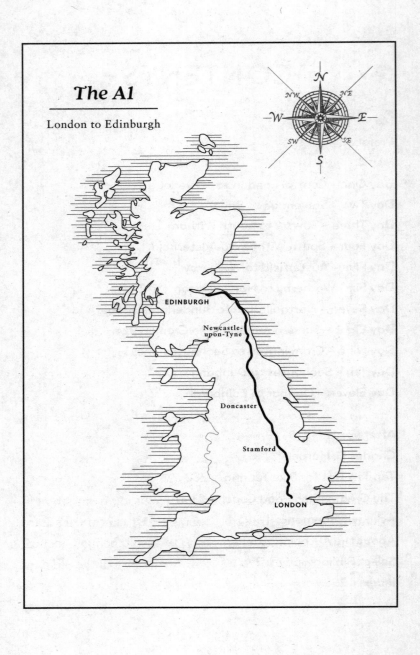

The A1

London to Edinburgh

EDINBURGH

Newcastle-
upon-Tyne

Doncaster

Stamford

LONDON

PREFACE

One hundred years ago, the most famous road in Britain ceased to exist. The Ministry of Transport had declared that numbers were the future, not names. So the Great North Road – the highway used down the ages by kings, queens, government troops, retreating rebels, pack horses, drovers, stage coaches, highwaymen, footpads, mail coaches, Penny Farthings and early motor cars – was quietly steered onto history's hard shoulder. In the summer of 1921, the A1 was born.

Under its new title, the old road has gone from strength to crash-barriered strength. Over the last century it's hard to remember a time when the A1 wasn't being widened, improved or upgraded. Now many a memory of the old days lies crushed beneath vast quantities of reinforced concrete and tarmac. More than half of the highway's 400 miles are effectively a motorway – the A1(M), a contradiction in terms.

Nonetheless, the original name has refused to die. Villagers from Hertfordshire in England to East Lothian in Scotland still talk about how *their* main road used to be part of a greater whole. At some deeper level the idea of a Great North Road remains embedded in the British psyche, even if the modern reality is rather more prosaic – an overcrowded bypass just to the west of Baldock, for example. Physical remnants survive too. There are stretches where the new has been built next to the old, rather than on top of it: an orphaned mile or so in locations such as Tempsford in Bedfordshire, Stilton in Cambridgeshire or Cromwell in Nottinghamshire. Stand on one of these forgotten high streets and it's remarkably easy to visualise a time when the mail coach was the king of the road – the horses' hooves clattering and the guard blowing his horn.

The Great North Road... Savour those four words. For reasons that I can't quite explain, the compass point is important. Which proper traveller can resist a road sign with a crisp, white arrow pointing to "The North" in no-nonsense sans-serif?

———

The concept of numbering roads had begun in France in the nineteenth century under Napoleon Bonaparte. André

Michelin, the founder of the tyre company, later became a fan of these "N" – or national – roads radiating from Paris. Once he had made the system more organised over there, he tried to persuade the British government to adopt it. After the First World War, he won over the Director-General of Roads in the newly created Ministry of Transport. By 1921 Sir Henry Maybury had decided to take the plunge. The top six highways would be spokes from London, the next three would have Edinburgh as their hub. There was some argument over the precise order. At one point the Portsmouth Road was going to be the A2 rather than the A3; similarly, the Bath Road would have been designated the A3 rather than the A4. But all agreed which road would be the first among equals. The Great North Road *had* to become the A1 – it was the longest, the grandest and the only one to run from capital to capital. It took a while for the system to catch on. Earlier in 1921 the *Berwickshire News* had confidently reported that the highway between London and Edinburgh was to be called "Road Number 1". However, by July civil servants were writing their memos and by October mapping companies were preparing to update their charts with the new A-road designations. In 1921, Britain bade farewell to The Great North Road.

———

My first experience of the A1 came as a 19-year-old student bound for Newcastle from London via the National Express coach service. With an elongated sports bag in one hand and a standard-issue 1980s ghetto-blaster in the other, I saw the road as never-ending and the coach as simply the cheapest way of getting from A to B.

Over the next four years I rode it, car-shared it, hitch-hiked it and drove it. I stopped at all the services and despaired at all the road works. But, slowly, the A1 started to seep into my soul. My first job was as a newspaper reporter in Darlington, using it to cover the misdemeanours of Catterick squaddies at Richmond Magistrates' Court or record the results of the "Best Cow with Calf at Feet" competition at a myriad of agricultural shows. Later, armed with a company car and a slightly better cut of suit, I patrolled the Peterborough patch as a regional TV reporter. All the time the A1 was expanding – eating up an ever-larger hinterland. Perhaps perversely, its quirks and its history were revealing themselves too. This wasn't a modern road suddenly imposed upon the landscape (like that American upstart Route 66…); it was the latest incarnation of a highway pieced together over centuries.

Now, fast forward a decade or two. I'd bought a bicycle and was out and about most weekends. Over the years the rides got longer and the machines got sleeker. Never a natural sportsman, I still managed my first 100-mile sportive – a glorious summer schlep around the lanes of Norfolk. So what should come next? A foreign jaunt? Land's End to John O'Groats? Or perhaps – after all these years – a return to the Great North Road, or "GNR" for short.

It remained just an idea for a while – classic pub talk. But then I came across the writings of Charles G. Harper – an author who had set out to do exactly the same thing more than a century ago. I did my research. Harper already had a string of articles and books to his name when he turned his attention to the Great North Road. Slightly old-fashioned and very conservative, he had explored the highways between London and the South Coast by foot, "tramping the roads with all the ardour of the old pilgrim" as he liked to tell friends. But now, with 400 miles in front of him, he knew he would have to resort to something more new-fangled – a bicycle. The roads were quiet. Mail coaches were long gone, both people and goods went by rail instead. Harper would cycle into towns where the high streets seemed too broad for the remaining traffic. Even the picturesque coaching inns were struggling to survive. Few foresaw that the motor car would soon give roads a new lease of life. But a sense of lost grandeur seemed to appeal to him.

"The story of the roads belongs to history, and history is, to your thoughtful man, quite as interesting as the best of novels," he declared.

Those words stirred something in me. The 100th anniversary of the introduction of the A1 was surely the perfect time to go on my own pilgrimage. And thanks to a Victorian gentleman with a trademark moustache and bow tie, I had found a hero as well as a guide book.

After that I moved quickly. I bought as old-fashioned a bicycle as I could find – a Jamis Aurora, complete with brown handlebar tape and full-length mudguards. It wasn't a road bike; it was sturdier than that. In fact the chap in the bike shop called it a tourer, which sounded suitably Harper-esque. Perhaps embarrassed by the fact that Jamis is an American marque, I made sure it came in British Racing Green and replaced the saddle with an expensive alternative from the famously English company Brooks – it's a B17 in honey brown for those who want to know. The single pannier was also expensive, but it attached to the frame with a satisfyingly crisp click. I then began to bemuse and amuse my cycling mates by getting into training mode, loaded up for a long journey even if we were only heading to the local greasy spoon. With or without the extra baggage, I needed to get acquainted with the bike, to make sure I understood its quirks – how it felt when I pedalled out of the saddle, the best combination of chainring and derailleur gears, and so on. It behaved itself beautifully. I was nearly there.

These days, motorists can drive from London to Edinburgh in seven or eight hours if they really want to. I was aiming for 11 days. I wouldn't travel on the modern A1 – even if it was legal to do so. But I would stick as close as I could to the old route – whether that was via traditional inns in town centres or bypassed fragments on country stretches. I hoped that an ever-expanding network of cycle paths would help too.

So, one Tuesday in May, I travelled down to London for a lunchtime Grand Départ. Along with both volumes of Harper's 1901 publication *The Great North Road*, I stowed a few spare clothes and rather more spare maps. If nothing else I was looking forward to travelling at a cyclist's pace, slow enough to notice how Britain subtly changes in character as one heads north – the landscape and the language, the architecture and the attitude.

This isn't a book about cycling, it's a book about a road. The Great North Road – undoubtedly the most romantic and most historic highway in the United Kingdom.

DAY ONE

CENTRAL LONDON TO STEVENAGE

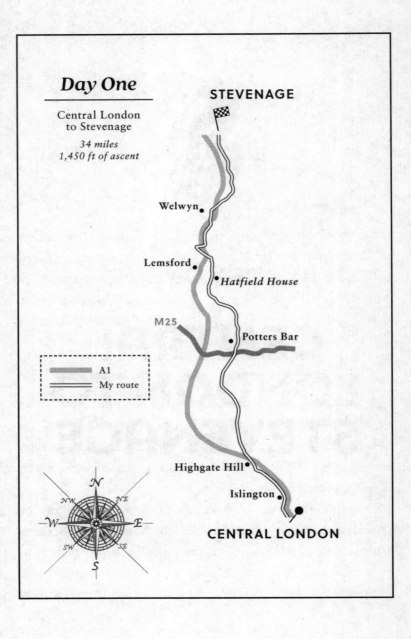

Day One

Central London
to Stevenage

34 miles
1,450 ft of ascent

STEVENAGE

Welwyn

Lemsford

Hatfield House

M25

Potters Bar

A1
My route

Highgate Hill

Islington

CENTRAL LONDON

N
NW   NE
W   E
SW   SE
S

A pedal has yet to turn and I've already cheated by about half a mile. I should be starting in a stubby little street behind St Paul's Cathedral by the name of St Martin's-le-Grand. This was where the mail coaches began their 400-mile journey to Edinburgh at a long-demolished General Post Office. Late Victorian cyclists, Harper tells us, took their cue from the coaches and began many record-breaking attempts from the same place.

But I've moved up Aldersgate and strayed onto Old Street where historical authenticity is losing out to the attractions of a twenty-first century flat white at a bike café. It goes by the excellent name of Look Mum No Hands. Might this be a better place to start?

Certainly the mix of bikes and baristas gives off an effortless London cool. To the left, a mechanic spins a wheel on his truing jig, adjusting a spoke. To the right, one of a posse of bearded coffee-makers gets the milk wand frothing. Twenty tyre-less wheels hang from the ceiling for no apparent reason, pleasant, jangly pop music plays in the background and coffee-table magazines with titles like "*Soigneur*" are strewn across wooden shelves. On the walls, the rainbow stripe colours worn on the jersey of cycling's world champion run like a demented dado rail. They even follow me into the loo. Nevertheless, I take a look at this happy hubbub and decide that as a starting line, it will do nicely.

Next, the formal photo. A mechanic loiters nearby and seems reasonably impressed with my plan. We head outside.

"Yeh, man, you're stoked for Edinburgh," he says as he snaps away.

… And then rather ruins his street-cred as I have to explain the finer points of air-dropping the photo from his phone to mine. But thank you, I needed that picture.

I go back to my table and empty my cup. Before I go, I reach for the first of Charles Harper's books, trying to imagine how he would have felt setting off on the same journey in 1900. In that era, motorised traffic was minimal. Looking back at his efforts in 1922 he remembered that:

People would still turn and gaze, interested, at a mechanically-propelled vehicle; and few were those folk who had journeyed the entire distance between London to Edinburgh in one of them… on any long journey you were never sure of finishing by car what you had begun.

The same goes for me by bike, I have to say. I've certainly never attempted anything this ambitious. The book is put away, the pannier gets secured and it's out onto the street before a right turn onto Goswell Road. Strange to say, I am completely undaunted by the task ahead. Have I worried in the build up? Yes. Have friends and family raised sceptical eyebrows? Certainly. But now, London to Edinburgh simply means immersing myself in a swirl of Hackney cabs and delivery vans. The bigger picture will have to wait, because this lot aren't taking any prisoners.

Windows, both retail and residential, flash by. Fast enough for individual details to be quickly erased, slow enough to gain an overall impression. Tourist London, it's clear, has been left behind. This is now a living, working London full of plumbers' suppliers, blocks of flats, even children playing, for heaven's sake.

Off, unseen to my left, is one of the few unchanging features across the centuries: Smithfield meat market, where drovers directing their herds once presented a serious hazard. Writers spoke of coaches competing for road space with unruly cattle – their horned faces sometimes scaring the horses as they loomed out of the thick London fog.

The junction at The Angel arrives quickly. The original pub which gave this part of Islington its name has long gone, but the Wetherspoon chain has done the obvious thing, creating another in roughly the same place. However, from my perspective, another inn further along the high street was more important. A painting from 1821 by the artist James Pollard entitled *North Country Mails at The Peacock* gives a clear sense of the bustle involved. This decade saw coaching near its zenith – and it shows in the detail. One coach is on the point of leaving, the driver drilling the horses with the subtle use of reins and the brute force of a whip. In the background three other coaches prepare for the off, each one packed – ladies in their bonnets and gentlemen in their top hats. Somehow the artist has imparted an air of urgent excitement to every detail. Coaching, it's clear, had glamour. When Harper was writing, it was a glamour his older readers would still have been able to remember.

> *Londoners and country-cousins alike were never weary of the spectacle of the smart coaches, the businesslike coachmen and the resplendent, scarlet-coated guards preparing to travel through the night, north, south, east or west, with his Majesty's mails.*

A complex network had sprung up in a generation. As a result Britain's roads had gone from being an embarrassment to a source of national pride. Each mail coach had a guard who was issued with a sealed time-piece, a blunderbuss and two pistols as well as the mailbags they swore to protect with their lives. The black and maroon livery was seen as being classier than the array of brightly coloured stage coaches with names like the *Tally-ho* and the *Trafalgar*. In 1820 one magazine totted up both the stage- and the mail-coach options. Apparently there were 1,500 opportunities to leave the capital over the course of a 24-hour period. All were agreed that the most prestigious mail of them all was the one which ran from London to Edinburgh, along the Great North Road.

The Peacock is long gone. But I eventually find a plaque to its memory above a German doner kebab restaurant. I stop and scribble down a few notes before something rather unusual happens: a stranger talks to me. To be fair, it's cyclist to cyclist, but still, this is London isn't it? She is a cycle courier for Uber Eats, her mountain bike fitted with what looks like a bread crate. She also carries two insulated bags, the larger of which could handle even the most outrageously sized pizza.

"You look lost," she says. "Where are you heading?"

"Edinburgh. I think it's in that direction."

"Edinburgh? What, Edinburgh in Scotland?"

She clearly doesn't believe me.

"Yes, Edinburgh in Scotland. But first I've got to do a bit of research on this…"

I drift to a halt mid-sentence, realising this is no time for a description of a nineteenth-century oil on canvas.

"Basically, I'm going that way," I conclude, hoping a declamatory statement with my left arm will do the job better than any words.

"Oh, right. OK. Good luck."

———

I try – and fail – to find a rhythm amid the traffic along Upper Street toward Highbury Corner. All my kit is in the one pannier on the near-side rear wheel. I don't feel unbalanced as such, but I'm still working out my precise width for tight squeezes. The driver of a number 19 bus has to keep overtaking me between stops and we're both equally grumpy about it. Then a skip-hire lorry brutally cuts me up, the irate man behind the wheel mouthing obscenities. On the plus side, the Great North Road is giving me the full Islington experience; Islington High Street, Islington College, Islington Green and the Islington Assembly Hall. Historically, all of the centres of law and order were on the right-hand side of the road while the drinking establishments were on the left. That just about remains the case, even if the pubs that once slaked the thirst of the drovers have often been replaced by restaurants with cuisines from across the globe.

Upper Street becomes the Holloway Road to the north of Highbury Corner and the number of artisan bakeries tails off quickly. The boundary between "hipster" and "old school" is drawn quite precisely for me by two contrasting cafés. At 105 Holloway Road, you'll find Vagabond N7, a stripped-back modern coffee house with the de rigueur delivery bike outside – simply for show, of course. Inside, hessian sacks hang from the wall and the espresso coffee bean isn't just isolated to a country – Tanzania – but to a specific farm – Isuto. It's then further subdivided into a "varietal". Bourbon, apparently. Seminars are advertised on post cards. Sample title: "Better than you know yourself – influence, fake news and your online self."

The Hope Workers' Café is three doors further north. The tea is cheap and as excellent as Vagabond's coffee. It's clear that both are classics in their own way. I sup away, silently rejoicing that each finds a niche in the melée of modern London. Here at The Hope, an Arsenal scarf hangs next to the counter, together with a sign saying "No Loitering – minimum charge £1.50 on match days." Eight wooden tables are lined up across the shop with matching round-backed chairs. If you told me they'd been there for 100 years I wouldn't argue. In fact, it would only need to be 120 years to put us back in Harper's own era at the turn of the last century. That thought makes me reach for his book.

"However delightful the Holloway Road may have been in the coaching age, it is in these crowded days a very commonplace thoroughfare indeed," he writes. "The long reaches of mean streets and sordid bye-roads combine with the unutterably bad road surface to render the exit from London anything but pleasurable."

"Sordid" feels very harsh these days. Busy, yes and undoubtedly densely populated. Full of people moving with that sense of urgency you only seem to get in capital cities – ever onward and upward.

The road surface too has improved; it's the quality of the air that feels "unutterably bad". I feel as if I have inhaled as many fumes in half an hour as in a previous year on the country lanes of Norfolk. Generally drivers give me plenty of room, helped by bike lanes and "respect" zones at the innumerable traffic lights. To my surprise, I'm having more problems with fellow cyclists – the MAMILs (Middle-Aged Men In Lycra) who silently overtake and undertake through the narrowest of gaps. I feel the need for a cycling equivalent of the "Man on!" cry in football; something short and snappy for the guy overtaking in a hurry. "Coming through!" anyone?

I seem to have been climbing ever since I left Old Street, but the gradient increases as I approach Highgate Hill. In the days of horse power this 120-metre-high lump of London clay proved a real impediment. So much so that in the early nineteenth century they tried to build a tunnel here – the word they used at the time was "archway". But the engineers got their sums wrong and the whole thing collapsed leaving the cutting we see today. Perhaps surprisingly considering the embarrassment, the whole area began to be called Archway. And the impressively high bridge carrying Hornsey Lane above the traffic shows how deep the navvies dug.

To avoid the modern dual carriageway I follow the cycle path up the original Highgate Hill – with the original gradient. It was at the bottom of this hill that a demoralised Dick Whittington famously paused as he heard Bow Bells ring out "Turn again Dick Whittington, thrice Lord Mayor of London". To my left is the Whittington Stone pub and in front of me, the Whittington Hospital. The man himself is remembered on the pavement with a monument but it all feels rather half-hearted. Where you might imagine a large statue of Dick in bronze, you'll simply find his cat in stone, all but obscured by protective iron railings. For a part of London that values its heritage it's a strange omission. And overhanging all this, an inconvenient truth: Whittington was a Gloucestershire lad. If he was trying to go home, what on earth was he doing heading north?

At the top, I can't resist a short diversion onto Hornsey Lane – just to see the road carried across the Archway cutting. From this vantage point, above the traffic, London is a magnificent sight. In the foreground the buses chug northwards, while in the distance the sun glints off the skyscrapers clustered on the horizon. A gaggle of cranes confirms that more whoppers are on their way.

In my mind's eye this was to have been the sort of gorgeous May day capable of topping up a tan. In reality it feels more like March, with the sun giving off surprisingly little heat. Stationary for too long, I realise that it's only kinetic exercise that's keeping me warm. Lengthy gawping at London landmarks isn't going to be good for the internal thermostat – or my average speed. Nevertheless I drink in the view one last time. For travellers heading south in the old days, this must have been the "wow" moment, even if it was a less lofty St Paul's Cathedral grabbing the spotlight.

Next, I plunge down North Hill where I somehow grind the chain off the front ring as I attempt to change gear too close to another red light. I curse my slowness at adapting to urban cycling as the bike gloves get their first film of grease. While the A1 now heads north west, I take the original Great North Road, the modern A1000. It's called the High Road through Finchley and up toward Barnet – I take "high" as an honorific title – a recognition of its mighty history.

At North Finchley the Tally Ho pub dominates a wedge-shaped junction. Tally Ho Corner was an early meeting point for the North Road Cycling Club – a sort of super-club for Victorian cyclists. It's difficult not to admire these pioneers. To join, you had to prove you had ridden 100 miles in a day – hard enough now, but even tougher in a world of basic bikes, dirt roads and non-pneumatic tyres. A book charting the first 50 years of the NRCC makes it clear that they used the Great North Road as their unofficial race track. It includes a glorious photo showing its members outside the Tally Ho in 1893. More than 40 cyclists pose with their conventional-looking bikes with just a couple of old timers hanging on to their "Ordinaries".

"The 'Good Old Ordinary'," reminisced the book's authors, "With what affection was it regarded by those who were masters (more or less!) of it, and how they rebelled against its eclipse by the dwarf bicycle!

"We never rode one ourselves – we were born a little too late – but it sends a wave of resentment through us to hear the modern generation referring to it as 'the penny farthing' – a term we positively refuse to use."

Progressing on my own "dwarf bicycle", Finchley becomes Whetstone and the world starts to feel greener. The houses are now 1930s semis and on the outskirts of Barnet there's also an elegant cinema from the same era. At Chipping Barnet, a parish church is curiously placed within a junction just before the main shopping street – a spiritual gateway to the world of Mammon. Then London ends. Abruptly. One minute there's the usual buzz around fast-food joints and dry-cleaning outlets, the next it's Hadley Green where horse chestnut candelabra sway in the wind, the smell of newly mown grass hangs in the air and a youngster on a trike pedals across the park to his grandad. I breathe in and realise I am taking my first proper gasp of non-metropolitan air. Soon afterwards, as if in response, a roadside sign announces that I'm in Hertfordshire, which is apparently "the County of Opportunity".

A little further on a fork in the road marks the point where the Edinburgh and Holyhead roads used to diverge, the latter heading toward St Albans. Within another mile I cycle under the M25 – another indicator that the big city is being left behind. It's a feeling Londoners have cherished for decades. When the crime writer Dorothy L. Sayers was writing her short story *The Cat in the Bag* in the 1920s – published in a collection of her tales entitled *Lord Peter Views the Body* – this particular stretch of road was an invitation to put your foot down:

"It is not known why motorists, who sing the joys of the open road, spend so much petrol every weekend grinding their way to Southend and Brighton and Margate... [when] all the time the Great North Road winds away like a long, flat, steel-grey ribbon – a surface like a race-track, without traps, without hedges, without side-roads, and without traffic. True, it leads to nowhere in particular; but, after all, one pub is very much like another."

Don't you just love the Southerner's disdain for anything or anyone north of Cambridge? Still, Sayers writes a good yarn. This one features her aristocratic detective Lord Peter Wimsey engaging in a motorbike chase between North London and Eaton Socon after a bag containing a woman's severed head slips from the back of a rider's bike near Hatfield. Just another Great North Road tale.

I cycle into Potters Bar, which tries to pretend it's still in London with a magnificently metropolitan bus garage. However, the high street feels a little forlorn, overshadowed since the railway had the temerity to build the station on the previously obscure Darkes Lane instead. Until now my brain has been kept more than busy with the ever-changing tableau around me, but that fizz seems to dissipate with the increasing gradient. I grunt and I wheeze myself up to the high ground around the radio transmitters of Brookmans Park, my gaze never leaving the road beneath my feet. Nevertheless, I needed that. I'm always the better for the first lung-buster of any ride.

As the country opens up on the approaches to Hatfield House, this really does feel like Hertfordshire. In fact, if you go back centuries, the stately home was the only reason there was a decent road in this part of the world. It wasn't until the nineteenth century that the Marquess of Salisbury bought himself a bit more privacy by moving the Great North Road westwards with the help of a canny three-way deal with the old turnpike trust and the new Great Northern Railway.

The building is still owned by the same family and that road exists as a track – visible behind locked gates and displayed on Google Maps. Several months earlier I'd cheekily asked if they would open them especially for me – in the interests of historical authenticity of course. They were very polite and kindly offered me a complimentary ticket to the House. But as for the gates, they were strictly for the use of "The Family". The Salisburys down the centuries are nothing if not consistent.

I present my ticket and wander through the grounds. The Hatfield estate was once owned by Henry VIII, who used it as a base for his three children – they would later become a hat-trick of sovereigns: Edward VI, Mary I and Elizabeth I. The Elizabethan era began when, while sitting under an oak tree, Elizabeth learned of her sister Mary's death. The House, which I guiltily clip-clop through in my cyclist's metallic cleats, was built a little later in 1611. It's a Jacobean triumph with rooms and paintings to take your breath away. Amid the grand portraits of long-dead marquesses, there are formal photos of the current generation of the same family. Robert Salisbury, the head of the family, also writes the foreword for a book celebrating the house's history. He doesn't mince his words about some of his ancestors:

"It is true that a number of them were distinguished servants of the Crown, but, particularly in the second half of the seventeenth century and for most of the eighteenth, far too many were as feckless and incompetent as they were stupid."

One Salisbury was so strapped for cash that he had to leave Hatfield for a smaller property near Baldock:

"There he lived surrounded by a rapacious mistress and a brood of illegitimate children. That Hatfield survived his incumbency is largely thanks to the loyalty and good sense of his wife... who kept the show on the road and enabled her son to enter into some sort of inheritance."

I walk with the bike – cycling is not permitted – past the surrounding parts of the Old Palace into the heart of Hatfield. Many a British stately home lies in isolation. Hatfield House manages that on three sides, but to the west it rubs up right against the town. I emerge onto pretty Fore Street, a steep thoroughfare that must have taxed coach drivers when it formed part of the main road. At the bottom there's a pub that I find impossible to pass by. The Eight Bells is a whitewashed building with a tall chimney totally out of proportion to everything else. Under the eaves, a notice proclaims its connection to *Oliver Twist*:

"This Eight Bells Inn is without doubt that small public house where Bill Sikes and his dog found temporary refuge after the brutal murder of Nancy. It was in the tap room that an antic fellow, half pedlar and half mountebank after mentioning bloodstains, offered to remove the stains from Sikes's hat."

It says something about how deep Dickens is buried in the national psyche that you'd be forgiven for thinking we were dealing with an historical event, rather than a novel. The pub seems to have become similarly embedded in the streetscape over the centuries and I have my swift half-pint sitting at a window where I am level with pedestrians' feet.

The next stretch had looked straightforward. After all, the street is still called The Great North Road as it passes Hatfield railway station. But then it suddenly disappears. Closer inspection reveals that it's jumped across the main line without bothering with a bridge. Yes, I had planned this section of the route back at home; no, I hadn't noticed this glaring anomaly. It turns out that there had been a bridge, but it had collapsed back in 1966. Eventually I find a pedestrian replacement brought in to assuage the locals, but all this gets me thinking rather more deeply. What exactly is the Great North Road? Is the Great North Road from one particular era purer than another? Is it the route, is it the tarmac, is it the modern name? I wasn't expecting such philosophical questions to arise so close to London.

The very next section puts me through my paces. The A1(M) snakes northwards, crossing the River Lea via an anonymous bridge. A busy B-road (bearing the GNR name) shadows it all the way. But I happen to know that an even earlier version of the road sidled further west to cross the Lea at Lemsford – initially via a ford. And even there I face a choice. The road used to wend its way due north along what is now a private tree-lined track. Am I to trespass in the name of sticking to the True Path?

I ponder these weighty issues while tucking into a plate of chips at The Sun pub, the bike locked to an ancient water pump in the back yard. With timeless cottages and a proprietorial heron fishing in the shallows, Lemsford has rolled back the years.

Two things are becoming clear. First, these unscheduled refreshment breaks are playing havoc with the timetable. I'm already aware of an internal dialogue between the "That looks interesting" devil and the "Keep on moving" angel. I wrestle with this dilemma for all of two minutes before deciding, with a dollop of ketchup, that the devil must win. I've got two weeks off work, my wife and kids are happy at home and I am in the very unusual position of being able to do whatever I want, without consequence. This is not a Land's End to John O'Groats race, it's a journey – a journey to be savoured.

Second, I will constantly have to choose between alternate routes. This has been a living, breathing road for centuries, so there's been layer upon layer of change. Clearly I can't take dual carriageways and I'm not wild about fast single-track A-roads either. But given the choice, I'll take the most historic Great North Road available. In summary: keep safe, go old.

The chips – never the food of champions – sit a little heavy in the stomach on the climb out of Lemsford and up Digswell Hill. The A1 is in its own cutting to my left but the old road takes me up over a summit and down into Welwyn – that's Welwyn the village as opposed to the garden city three miles to the south. Welwyn is the first of many places along the route with which I fall head-over-heels in love. I'm not sure why, but I hadn't expected it to happen so close to London. It's a pukka coaching village which looks utterly timeless. The big landowners here were too snooty to have anything to do with the railway in the nineteenth century, so while Potters Bar and Brookmans Park embraced the steam age, this place turned its back.

"Street and houses face you alarmingly as you descend the steep hillside," wrote Harper, "wondering (if you cycle) if the sharp corner can safely be rounded, or if you must needs dash through door or window of The White Hart, once one of the two coaching inns of the village."

I arrive in the same way down the same hill, but perhaps with better brakes. The White Hart still looks in fine fettle, as does The Wellington on the high street. I then turn right into Church Street where a cast-iron milestone tells me I'm 25 miles from London. *Four 25s in a 100, four 100s in 400*; there's something about long-distance cycling that makes you want to sub-divide and rationalise. *Twenty-five miles means I'm one-sixteenth of the way there*, I think to myself. Roughly. Very roughly as it turns out.

After Welwyn, the Great North Road follows a Roman route heading through dormitory suburbs. The area around Mardley Hill was later renowned as a haunt of highwaymen – there's still a Robbery Bottom Lane to prove it. But as I breast another hill a different vista awaits – Stevenage, my destination for the night. I pass the ancient Roebuck pub, mentioned by all the history books as being some distance from what we now call Stevenage Old Town. These days it's been swallowed up in the conurbation, but it's still there – Airbnb customers being just the latest generation of travellers wanting the same old thing – a bed and a bite to eat. Then it's up past the delightfully named Roaring Meg shopping complex to the town centre where the Great North Road disappears under the strict grid pattern of this post-war new town.

I mooch around some underpasses in a slightly shifty manner, trying to find evidence of the old days. Thank goodness I've got the bike; without it I would look even more suspicious. After ten minutes I'm rewarded with a "Eureka" moment near the Six Hills Roundabout. The highway might not have survived but there's a solitary hedge running alongside the leisure centre. It undoubtedly marks one side of the original Great North Road. I suspect you can't really make a hedgerow verge Grade II listed, but I do hope no one is ever tempted to grub it up.

A stone's throw away, my Ibis hotel is best described as adequate. They let me take the bike to the room, but the lift is so tiny that I have to wheelie it in – the front wheel almost touching the ceiling. But because I forget to take the pannier off first, both man and bike collapse in a heap in front of the receptionist. Never a good look. For my evening meal I walk to the Old Town where the nineteenth-century buildings feel very higgledy-piggledy compared to their newer neighbours – as if an Old England theme park has been parachuted in by mistake.

After fish and chips I walk back, again looking for relics. I discover, to my horror, that part of the Great North Road suffers the indignity of being buried under a Tesco car park. Tomorrow, surely, the road will be treated with more respect.

DAY TWO

STEVENAGE TO SAWTRY

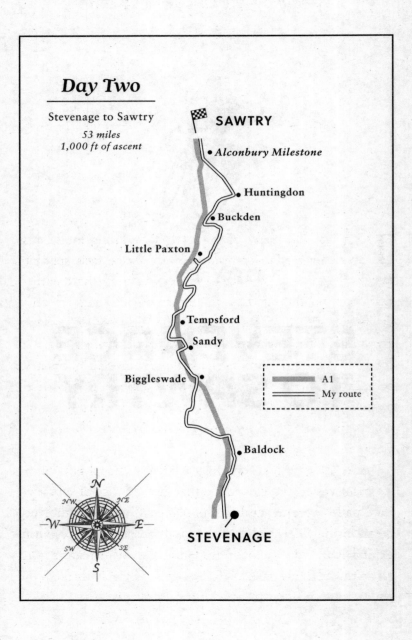

Day Two

Stevenage to Sawtry

53 miles
1,000 ft of ascent

SAWTRY

• *Alconbury Milestone*

• **Huntingdon**

• **Buckden**

Little Paxton •

• **Tempsford**

• **Sandy**

Biggleswade •

A1
My route

• **Baldock**

STEVENAGE

N
NW · NE
W · E
SW · SE
S

To a lad who grew up on a 1960s housing estate, just about every part of residential Stevenage feels spookily familiar: every cul-de-sac, every alley, every hard-earned additional porch. Exploring the endless avenues and crescents the previous evening, the lyrics to *The Sound of the Suburbs* came unbidden into my mind. The Members' hit from 1979 cornered the market in anger for those who had nothing to be angry about. Stevenage fits the bill – a thoroughly civilized place where, nevertheless, Johnny might be upstairs giving the neighbours some gyp with his "punk rock electric guitar". Cue: raucous riff.

Due to the fact that Stevenage is such a model new town, it's much easier to cycle around than my old slice of suburbia. Bike paths were integral to the planners' vision, with every detail lovingly chronicled at the local museum. My favourite exhibit is a 1948 public information film which starts with an animated figure called Charley cycling happily through the wide streets of a new town with the opening words:

"My, this is a grand way to start the day. Bit different to how it used to be, I can tell you."

Charley in New Town then shows a flashback of a previous life in the capital where, through cartoon fog, we're told in gentle Cockney that "it took a bloke a good hour to get to work".

In the Promised Land the commute would be quicker. Stevenage was divided into six neighbourhoods, each with its own facilities, each within easy distance of the dedicated industrial zone. Under the leadership of town planner Eric Claxton, more than 26 miles of cycle ways were built in the late 1950s and 1960s, allowing cars, bikes and pedestrians to be kept completely separate. His plan worked. Soon more than 40 per cent of people were using the paths to get to work or school. As such, the town even featured in a 1970s Ladybird book called *The Story of the Bicycle*. But despite these near-perfect cycling conditions, Stevenage still got a taste for the motor car. Claxton retired in 1972 with an OBE and an MBE for his efforts. At roughly the same time his colleagues were starting to widen many of the roads to cater for car journeys that, on paper at least, shouldn't have been necessary. Claxton had done everything right and the tide still turned. For some cultural reason that I can't begin to fathom, cycling became as deeply unfashionable then as it is achingly hip now.

New Town idealism feels in short supply as I start Day Two. The dominant view from my hotel window is the concrete slab of an empty BHS store. As I head out I'm greeted by two homeless people under multi-coloured sleeping bags. It's grey, windy and colder than I thought – time to rustle through the pannier for another base layer, rather than the topographical wisdom of Mr Harper.

I have breakfast in the Old Town before joining the commuter traffic. Then it's Graveley, with its two neighbouring pubs and a stage coach proudly displayed on the village sign. The landscape around Graveley will define my day. I keep on climbing and descending windswept hills, never far from – and often within sight of – the modern A1 in its gradient-free cuttings; close enough to smell the burning rubber from the HGVs. I'm starting to notice that I'm becoming aware of every single change in elevation. On a bike you feel every hill you're grinding up and you pine for every easier alternative. It's the vertical equivalent of the grass always being greener.

My first proper stop is at Baldock, a town which, unlikely as it may sound, takes its name from Baghdad. Baldock was basically a medieval Stevenage – a new town created in about 1140 by the Knights Templar. This mysterious order of warrior-priests saw Baghdad as an idealised city and named their community accordingly. The Latinised form of Baghdad is "Baldac", which has been mangled to "Baldock" over the centuries. It prospered in the coaching era and it's easy to spot what they call "carriage arches" surviving within both pubs and private houses – masquerading as converted garages, converted into central foyers and, occasionally, out and proud as passageways to hidden courtyards.

One magnificent specimen has tall, studded wooden doors looking for all the world as if they belong to Hampton Court or Harry Potter's Hogwarts. In all, I count 18, the finest example slightly off my intended route in Church Street. In this sixteenth-century house it feels as if every window has been shoved aside to make way for the central feature – two storeys worth of empty space. Surely a modern estate agent's worst nightmare.

In Baldock the Great North Road is only the second-oldest thoroughfare. It's trumped by the Icknield Way scything its way across England from Wiltshire to Norfolk. This route mostly sticks to the high ground across the Berkshire Downs and the Chilterns – a classic ridgeway, though historians argue as to its precise age and purpose. Some see evidence of an ancient trading route dating back more than 4,000 years. Others point to the mysterious absence of tracks in some places and the curious presence of ditches blocking its path in others. Here we find layer upon layer of history, open to many an interpretation.

As if in obeisance, the GNR turns first right and then left, temporarily losing its identity to the older road. On the first corner is The George, on the second The Old White Horse and – in between – the now-defunct Rose and Crown. These three inns used to carve up the coaching traffic between them. These days The George helpfully displays an old timetable on the wall of its front bar. Baldock was quite a transport hub. The *Perseverance* ran to Boston, the *Rockingham* to Leeds, the *Express* to Lincoln, the *Regent* to Stamford and the *Highflyer* to York. The more prestigious mail coaches ran from The White Horse – which feels surprising given the modern pub. I look at it more closely – a small building marooned in a large car park. Further investigation reveals that most of the inn complex burned down in the 1860s. The surviving pub was only the tap room – a far cry from the glory days.

It's worth saying that mail coaches didn't develop gradually over the years; they were the brainchild of one man, a businessman from the West Country. John Palmer owned two theatres, one in Bath and the other in Bristol. As a result he was a regular user of stage coaches and had grown frustrated by how long the Post Office took to deliver letters across similar distances. At that time the Post Office relied on so-called post boys – although they were often slightly dozy men. They travelled on horseback with varying degrees of initiative and intelligence. Not only were they slow, they were also either at the mercy of highwaymen or even in league with them.

Palmer's solution was devastatingly simple; give up on the post boys and carry the mail on fast coaches with armed guards. The new system would rely on precision timing and a regular supply of horses at strategically placed inns. The Post Office establishment fought Palmer every inch of the way, but he won through, establishing a service from Bristol to London in 1784. It was instantly successful, with many other cities following suit the following year. By 1786, The York Mail was in place – with The White Horse inn a crucial piece of its Great North Road network.

Like the horses, I labour up a moderately steep incline to the border with Bedfordshire. This is a watershed moment. From now on the rivers no longer flow south into the Thames, but east into the Wash. The main road too changes character. For drivers, Hertfordshire had appeared lush and green with barely a building to be seen, but the A1(M) loses its brackets when it crosses the county boundary and suddenly it's a warts-and-all carriageway. People still actually live and trade on this stretch – that's almost a novelty now that so many of the miles between London and Newcastle have been upgraded. It would be a push to say that it feels like the ancient Great North Road, but if you really pay attention you can find fragments – curving cul-de-sacs for example, showing where the old route went before the modernisers got their rulers out. The author and former Great North Road trucker Chris Cooper brilliantly characterises these as the ox-bow lakes of the A1.

I've found a better rhythm today. It's as if my muscles have acclimatised to the extra effort the weight of the pannier requires. But from Junction 10, the modern A1 and the old Great North Road are one and the same, so I need to find an alternative. I endure a scary stretch of the A507 until Stotfold where I hit a proper bike route.

The cycle paths here are particularly hypnotic because distance is measured in time rather than, well, distance. That has to be wrong, but here I find it childishly addictive. Can life for a cyclist get any sadder than trying to get to Arlesey in fewer minutes than the signs dictate? Perhaps as a result I go astray, ending up at Arlesey's railway station as an InterCity train flashes by. Those guys will make Edinburgh by tea-time; I'll be happy with Cambridgeshire. I lug my bike across the footbridge and then find the Hiz – the first of my Wash-bound rivers – before switching to the Ivel, following its valley northward through the unfussy yellow-brick villages of Henlow and Langford.

At Biggleswade I am instantly charmed by a bustling market square and a small-town buzz. I also meet up with my mate Jim, who combines Saturday morning bike rides in Norfolk with longer motorcycle journeys when he gets the chance.

I almost don't recognise him with the crash helmet on.

"Good to see you," he says, removing it at last. "But I need proof for everyone else."

He points at my bike: "Go and do that again, right round the market square. I want all this on video."

I do as I'm told before we sit down for coffee. The Surfin Café has the best views in town and once had a killer quote from the author Terry Pratchett on its website. "Coffee is a way of stealing time that should by rights belong to your older self." I'm not entirely sure I ever knew what this meant, but I like it nonetheless. Inside, everyone seems to know everyone else and the guy behind the counter is the first to have ever offered me ice when he fills up my water bottle. Thank you, sir.

I've come to realise that places like this are the modern inn, providing me with my every need. Food and drink of course, but power and wi-fi too. But my mains cable only works if I balance it at a certain angle on the table. Gadget man Jim hangs his head at the spectacle.

"That's never going to last till Edinburgh. You get going, I'll find you some decent kit."

I look at my watch and realise that an hour has gone effortlessly by. I've committed the cardinal sin of bike touring – I've got too comfortable in one place.

We arrange to meet an hour or so up the road while I chase the memory of Biggleswade's most famous son – Dan Albone. A born inventor, Albone patented designs for everything from a very early tractor to an automatic potato planter. But he started off with bicycles. Look around Biggleswade and you'll see suspiciously old-fashioned bike frames installed as places to lock up their modern equivalent. Each one is engraved with "Ivel Works" – the factory Albone established here in the 1880s. On the bank of the river, he built up his business through an inquiring mind and force of personality. I love his story because I fear that the modern Albone would have hopped on the train to do something cool in London, while the Victorian original could flourish in Biggleswade – and have London's cyclists come to him.

Necessity might be the mother of invention, but timing helps too. Albone saw all the major developments in the design of the bicycle between his birth in 1860 and his death in 1906. He was presented with his first Boneshaker at the age of nine. These early machines, with pedals directly attached to the front wheel, were famously uncomfortable. By 1870 they were being replaced by Penny Farthings. Albone had built one of these for himself by the time he was 13. Then, in the 1880s, the Safety Bicycle came along with two revolutionary innovations. Most obviously the wheels were of a similar and modest size so that falling off didn't mean you were likely to break an arm or a leg. But this breakthrough was only possible because of another: a chain drive meaning that a large front sprocket was linked to a smaller one next to the back wheel. This multiplied the revolution of the pedals, dividing the effort required. In other words, it was pretty much the modern bicycle. Against big names elsewhere, Albone produced a steady supply of reliable bikes used by record-breaking cyclists across the country. In modern terms, products like the Ivel Light Roadster were cool, sleek and niche.

I've now seen an Albone information panel in the pub, his bike frames in the market place and a plaque on Shortmead

Street, so it's no surprise to bid the town goodbye via the official Dan Albone Car Park – complete with tractor sculpture. Let no one be in any doubt that Biggleswadians have got themselves a hero.

———

I cross the Ivel next to a large superstore. Without really meaning to, I bodge my way north directly alongside the dual carriageway using a mixture of proper pavements and soft verges. The hinterland of the Bedfordshire A1 is not an inspiring place to be: mangy-looking kerb-side rabbits, squashed purple coffee cups and ripped plastic bags caught on the spikes of stunted hawthorn trees. A couple of lay-bys provide relief, with one of them containing an entire hamlet – Lower Caldecote. Hidden under the trees I find the 46th milestone from London, picked out with paving stones and given as much reverence as if it were a war memorial. Nice work Caldecotians.

I start mile 47 from behind a hedge, bumping across a ploughed field. This is where you certainly need a tourer rather than a road bike – there's no way their super-skinny tyres could handle this. It's also a sort of trespass I suppose, but I'm still surprised to be approached by a police officer as I re-join the road near a garden centre.

"Excuse me sir, have you seen anyone acting suspiciously on these fields?" asks the PC.

What, apart from me? I haven't, but it quickly transpires that a number of "illegals" have escaped from a Hungarian HGV packed with plants and garden furniture. Police swarm over the lorry while a driver pulls up in the next lay-by. He *has* seen three people running through the fields. After texting Jim with the gossip, I pause to consider how many stowaways have first touched down on British soil alongside the Great North Road over the years.

I'm now on a proper strip of pavement approaching the settlement of Beeston; a place that had always caught my eye when I've sped past as a motorist. It's one of those places which the upgraded A1 simply bulldozed through in the 1960s with little regard for property or privacy. It used to be a hamlet on the southern fringes of the town of Sandy. Now most of its residents lie on the wrong side of four lanes of traffic. There is a footbridge – it's one of a number along this stretch. But together they form little more than a guilty penance from planners who must have realised they were wrenching communities apart.

So what's it like to live *on* the modern A1? After moving here from the other side of Bedfordshire, Gilly Lacey is perhaps typical of a new breed. Her house is a former pub, The Beeston Cross, which served GNR travellers until approximately 2005. I've effectively cold-called Gilly but, despite my ambush, I'm treated with as much hospitality as if this were still an inn. She's delighted with the extra bang she got for her buck.

"We love living here, we've got so much more space than we had before," she tells me. "And, listen, you can't really hear the traffic, can you?"

It's true. With decent double glazing there's a background hum, but nothing more. Gilly has photos on the wall showing her house in the old days. Then, the pub sign was on the other side of the road – probably where today's central reservation lies. But it's another picture which really takes my eye. It shows 15 cyclists lined up next to The Beeston Cross in a position which would now see them mown down by traffic. When I looked at it the first time I was surprised to see one of the 15 apparently climbing on the backs of two of his friends. On closer inspection he is in fact perched high on a Penny Farthing. The caption reveals that this is Sandy Cycling Club in all its glory. Like the Tally Ho photo it comes from that "crossover" period when a few die-hards were still out there, refusing to abandon the taller bikes.

From Gilly's, I cross the footbridge of guilt onto riverside meadows. Sandy wasn't really a Great North Road town, it lies a solid half-mile to the east and perhaps that's why its centre lacks a little of Biggleswade's soul. However, it is the home of the Bedfordshire Clanger – so well worth another detour. The clanger looks a little like an elongated sausage roll, but is actually a suet crust pastry. Crucially it has a meat filling at one end and something sweet at the other – two courses in one "package". It dates back to the nineteenth century when women made it for their menfolk labouring in the fields.

Really, the clanger's survival and current popularity is thanks to Gunns Bakery in the market square. David Gunns dates its revival to a one-off Bedfordshire Festival held nearby in the early 1990s.

"I was asked to set up a bakery for the festival. We baked Bedfordshire Clangers and they were queuing up halfway down the road for them," he told me. "We sold them in their hundreds."

Since then he has expanded the range and marketed them as a symbol of the county. If you're on a town-twinning trip to Europe you *will* want your town's name written along a clanger as your parting gift. For any sort of open-air event the clanger will be your festival food. You can even get them by mail order.

The one I enjoy at his café has gammon, potato and onion at one end and stewed apple at the other. There is, I'm told, a slim pastry boundary, although you've got to be careful not to get two courses in one mouthful. How do you tell which end is which? Two tiny holes punched in the pastry indicate meat; three slits means dessert.

David packs me off with two varieties from an ever-expanding list; lamb & jam and the Bombay Clanger – vegetable curry and mango. And I can honestly say that I ate nothing else until the evening. In the old days clangers were prized for their high calorific value. They still should be.

"Just finally," adds David, with a twinkle in his eye, "it's David Gunns, not Gunn. The way to remember is that Gunns's Bun-ses are the One-ses."

———

I retrace my tracks through Sandy to Girtford, but run out of luck on the A1 proper. After exploring a few dead ends I chance upon a gravel track along an abandoned railway embankment. The sun comes out in time to appreciate the beautiful village of Blunham with its timber-beamed houses and thatched cottages. Jim reappears and gives me the full motorcycle escort into Tempsford – the first place where I feel as if I am truly stepping back in time. We approach the village from the south along the original Great North Road. The church of St Peter is dressed in alternate layers of sand and ochre-coloured bricks. Officially, it's called "ironstone, cobbles and clunch" – clunch being a chalky limestone. An old pub called The Wheatsheaf is still there, as are the fifteenth-century beams on Gannock House, once an inn in its own right.

But a closer look reveals how much havoc the modern A1 has wreaked. When the land for the dual carriageway was compulsorily purchased in the early 1960s, the entrance gates to Tempsford Hall were left marooned on the wrong side of the road. Further north the village hall had been built right next to the main road and was surely the residents' pride and joy when it was completed in 1924. Now it couldn't be in a worse place. Finally, there's the fate of the Anchor Lodge. Once a village pub, it's now the Vanilla Alternative – a self-confessed venue for swingers. A pub which had long relied on a combination of locals and passers-by, it now trades on the easy anonymity of the big bad trunk road.

Thankfully none of this stops the residents from honouring the past and enjoying the present.

In 2000, the scrub behind the old Tempsford Hall gate became the Tempsford Millennium Garden Sanctuary, a peaceful little copse, once you've learned to tune out the traffic noise over the fence. More recently, monuments have been dedicated to members of the special forces who were flown out from here for undercover operations during the Second World War. The Royal Air Force base was designed to look like agricultural buildings. If you were in the know it was RAF Tempsford; everyone else thought it was Gibraltar Farm. Jim and I examine an obelisk unveiled by Prince Charles in 2013. At its heart is a mosaic featuring a dove flying by the light of the moon.

"To honour and remember the women who went out from RAF Tempsford and other airfields and ports to aid resistance movements in occupied Europe 1941–45. Some remain nameless. Some did not return."

I read it twice, letting the words sink in. Yes, this is a monument specifically to honour the women involved in this most risky of missions. Of the 75 named, the accompanying website makes clear that 29 were arrested – and 16 of them were executed. One more chose to use her suicide pill, while two more died in captivity.

"You'd never know any of this was here, would you?" says Jim, gesturing at the hundreds of cars roaring past on the A1 behind us.

There's also a haunting poem written by the cryptologist Leo Marks – something of a Special Operations Executive legend. He wrote it after learning that his fiancée had been killed in an air crash in Canada. Entitled "The Life That I Have", it has become a popular verse at funerals in recent years. And even here – unspoken on a block of stone – the simplicity of the language emphatically articulates the depth of his grief.

———

Jim heads back to the A1 while I continue directly north. The old Great North Road joins its current incarnation at the Anchor Lodge where another of those guilt-ridden overpasses takes me high above the traffic so that I at least imagine I can see the smaller River Ivel joining the larger Great Ouse in the distance. I end up exactly where I want to be: close enough to the A1 to understand the lie of the land, but far enough away for traffic noise to be but a distant thrum. I head uphill toward Little Barford on the trunk road as it crosses the now-conjoined rivers. Motorists heading south use a modern bridge; traffic heading north streams over one from the turnpike era, patched and repaired, but largely the same as when it was built in the early 1700s. In between, there's the no-man's land of the Kelpie Marine Boatyard. Only non-motorway sections of the A1 tolerate such idiosyncratic backwaters – an oasis of boats and boat people surrounded by the roar of the road. When traffic backs up from the Black Cat Roundabout, drivers wanting to rush are forced to look down on others whose lives are running at a very different speed.

Meanwhile, I'm up on the high road heading past farms to reach the border with Cambridgeshire. There's a perfectly direct way through St Neots from here, but it was never the Great North Road. So that purist urge (I've labelled it the "Lemsford Doctrine" after yesterday's angel/devil dilemma in the village of Lemsford) makes me add two miles to the total by heading back to Eaton Socon. My reward is a view of The White Horse coaching inn, made famous by a cameo role in Charles Dickens's *Nicholas Nickleby* where the village is thinly disguised as "Eton Slocomb".

I cross the Great Ouse again at St Neots and traverse the river for the third time on my way to Little Paxton. It's only then that I realise I have been valley-hopping all day. First, the Hiz from Henlow, then the Ivel around Biggleswade and finally the Great Ouse. In each case the former has flowed into the latter so that there's now a fair head of water streaming toward The Wash. On a smaller scale, today's route has reproduced what the GNR does throughout its 400-mile journey – pragmatically jumping from valley to valley, joining and then leaving Roman roads where necessary, but always trending toward due north and low gradients.

I'm now heading for a short loop of the original Great North Road in honour of a seemingly trivial event which had the most serious implications for cycling in the UK. The date was 21 July 1894 and the North Road Cycling Club was holding one of its traditional 50-mile races. These could be chaotic affairs, but at the time just three cyclists were racing along a straight section of the road near the 57th milepost at Little Paxton when they approached a horse and trap. One of them, F. T. Bidlake, saw the reins in the lap of the driver. His recall of events was quoted in S. H. Moxham's 1935 book *Fifty Years of Road Riding – A History of the North Road Cycling Club*:

"Seeing us she lifted the reins; unfortunately she pulled the wrong one and the chariot drew across our track. We all three swung onto the grass verge on our left, but the obedient horse got there before us, and we ruined our cycles and retired, but no harm was done to the horse or carriage or its occupants. The lady, however, made her lament, and the police issued a general proclamation that racing must cease."

It was an incident where the driver was at fault but it's no exaggeration to say that the ramifications for cyclists reverberated down the decades. There had been occasional clashes before, as well as altercations with the police. But for reasons that no one can quite explain, this incident provoked a moral panic – with cyclists as the bad guys. Within three years the National Cyclists Union had voluntarily banned all road racing in the United Kingdom. Presumably similar incidents were happening in other European countries at the same time. But no other nations took against road racing like the people of Britain. Instead, we turned to time-trials.

Ned Boulting, in his 2013 book *On the Road Bike*, describes the result superbly:

"It was to be a path of separate development, involving semi-clandestine, early-morning starts or else hammering in isolation up and down dual carriageways.

"The British Isles, in cycling terms, had become the Galapagos Islands. Its indigenous species were evolving into something unique and endangered..."

Strangely enough, it was Bidlake who emerged as the man laying down the new rules. Much overlooked, there is actually a memorial to him back at Girtford, close to a venerable old bridge across the Ivel. His club mates put it there because it was one of the favourite locations for those clandestine starts. Decades later, in a 1969 article for the winter edition of the *Bedfordshire Magazine*, writer Ronald English remembered those early mornings with fondness:

"'Fullers' resthouse at Girtford would be astir when we arrived. There was always a strong smell of embrocation, and men dressed in black tights and cotton or alpaca jackets were preparing their cycles, fitting sprint wheels and removing mudguards."

The white-haired figure of Bidlake, says English, would be found close by with a North Road Cycle Club badge on his lapel and a watch in his hand. He was clearly adored within this tight-knit community. The memorial stone speaks of his "singular charm and culture" while the notice board alongside describes him as "an outstanding administrator and meticulous timekeeper".

———

In Little Paxton I scuff around in the undergrowth at the junction of Mill Lane looking for the crucial 57th milestone. Roadside detective work is a faff by bike. You've got to lose the gloves, find the right map and then protect it against an ever-present wind. Ordnance Survey marks an "MS", but I can't locate it. Then I notice it shows another one, just a few hundred yards south. I leave aside the fact that milestones shouldn't be so close, because this one is easily found, even amid the nettles and the cow parsley. It's so weathered that I can only make out the words "London", "Lt Paxton" and "Miles" on its pock-marked face. The earth has been scoured deep around its foundations, but it stands firm and I'm sure this is the one. I can't resist calling it a milestone in the history of British cycling.

I head back across the flood meadows of Great Paxton, Offord D'Arcy and Offord Cluny before another Lemsford Doctrine tack takes me toward Buckden. Bypassed by the modern A1, it's pleasantly sleepy – a Cambridgeshire Welwyn if you like. There's a religious flavour too, thanks to the surviving parts of a palace once owned by the Bishops of Lincoln. Many a monarch stayed here and it was also used by Henry VIII as a place to effectively imprison his first queen – Catherine of Aragon was kept under house arrest during Henry's three-year marriage to his second wife, Anne Boleyn. Most of the palace has long-since disappeared, but the reddest of walls and The Great Tower survive – you can't beat tall Tudor brickwork for a sense of majesty. Add the melancholy of a spurned queen and Buckden certainly has a story to tell.

I take a breather in the churchyard and take in the view. As I'm off the bike, I can admire that too. Even leaving aside the pannier, this tourer is heavier than my road bike back home and clunkier too. On conventional racers you change gear with a sidewards flick of the brake lever – slick when they work, but fiddly to fix. Instead, I have stubbier levers on the end of my handlebars. These "bar end shifters" have already delighted one old boy in Sandy who told me his bike had them in the 1950s. They're doing me proud too, responding, I notice, to the subtlest nudge of either palm. Elsewhere the leather runs smooth on the saddle and the pannier's behaving itself. Let's not jinx it, but man and bike appear to be in perfect harmony.

The place to stay in Buckden is probably The George, a coaching inn which has reinvented itself as a boutique hotel, complete with 12 notable Georges on its pub sign. Residents get to stay in rooms named after Orwell, Best, Bernard Shaw, Stubbs, Washington, Handel, Stephenson, Gershwin, Eliot, Mallory, Harrison and King George I.

Harper liked Buckden, describing it as a village which must have had high hopes of growing into a town – until the railways took the coaching trade away:

> Nowadays The George is all too large for its trade, and a portion of it is converted into shops. As for the interminable rooms and passages above, they echo hollow to the infrequent footfall, where they were once informed with the cheerful bustle and continuous arrival and departure.

Well, Charles, you'll be glad to know the twenty-first century sees it cheerful once more.

Moving on, the high street quickly morphs into the A1 but thankfully a pavement takes me alongside the traffic to Brampton before I head into Huntingdon as the evening rush hour bites. Huntingdon was the birthplace of Oliver Cromwell and this town is the first of many close to the Great North Road with English Civil War connections. The Cromwell Museum is contained within the remains of his old school at one end of the high street. It's small, compact and studiously neutral on the question of whether their man was a Good Thing or not. Recently refurbished (and reopened by that old roundhead Sir John Major) it explores the man and his times sympathetically and thoughtfully. The country was split geographically by the conflict – in general the north and west were for the king, while south and east were for Parliament. At several junctures that put the GNR on the front line. Indeed as I travelled further north it often felt as if the ghost of the Lord Protector was following me around.

Whatever time I approach Huntingdon by car, it always seems to be jammed with traffic. But a few decent cycle paths mean that this time I can escape quickly toward Alconbury Hill. The Great North Road here always had a reputation. The hill was steep, the landscape bleak and the chance of daylight robbery consequently high. In R. C. and J. M. Anderson's 1973 book *Quicksilver: A Hundred Years of Coaching 1750–1850,* the authors talk of a place called Stonegate Hole "shut in by dense woods" which provided the perfect cover for both highwaymen – who rode horses – and footpads, who robbed on foot. When this hollow was later filled in, navvies found skeletons thought to be "the relics of unfortunate travellers". This is where the mail coach's armed guard earned his money. Dressed in bright-red greatcoats and only too keen to make a racket on a coaching horn, these men provided a high-profile deterrent, backed up by two pistols and a substantial blunderbuss.

For "bleak" then, read "dull" now. The road might run parallel to the modern A1, but that doesn't stop drivers attempting to reach the same speeds on the old road – with us cyclists suffering in their wake. Even spotting a family of red kites gliding on the thermals does little to lift my mood. I concentrate on my posture – don't hunch over. And my breathing – deep and slow. A steady 14 mph will do nicely. But high on the hill, there is time to pay homage to one of the great monuments of the road – the milestone at Alconbury. In fact "milestone" doesn't remotely do justice to this 5-foot-tall chunk of sandstone. The coachmen used to call it "the obelisk" – which sounds much grander. Originally it marked the place where the Great North Road joined the Old North Road – an alternative route from London which started at Shoreditch and continued through places like Tottenham, Enfield and Waltham Cross. Harper describes the junction in characteristically vivid language:

The summit of this convenient Golgotha is the place where the North Road and the Great North Road adjust their differences, and proceed by one route to the North... Travellers coming south could have a choice of routes to London from Alconbury Hill, as the elaborate old milestone still standing at the parting of the ways indicates, showing 64 miles by way of Huntingdon, Royston, and Ware and four miles longer by the way we have come.

Whisper it to *Great* North Road fanatics, but the *Old* North Road actually has the better pedigree since it's based on Ermine Street – the Roman road connecting London with Lincoln. As late as the stagecoach era it was the GNR's equal, carrying dozens of coaches every day. But by the 1960s the tide had turned. The southern section had found a new life as the A10, but the stretch north of Royston became the obscure A1198. Its downgrade came at the same time as extra lanes and millions of pounds were being lavished on the A1. The medieval upstart had finally trounced the Roman thoroughbred.

As a result, today's Old North Road is wonderfully unimproved. Hefty roadside oaks and chestnuts speak of the road's antiquity and an old gibbet survives at Caxton Gibbet – even if it's now really only a gimmick for the eponymous retail park. But without a dual carriageway to its name, this ancient thoroughfare provides a tantalising glimpse of how the Great North Road would once have looked.

I'd trained by doing as many 50-mile days as I could, but they were normally quick morning affairs with the minimum of stops. Cycling and exploring take much longer, I realise.

As a weak sun dips to the horizon somewhere in Northamptonshire, I'm starting to regret getting comfortable in Biggleswade. Thankfully, the Alconbury obelisk is my summit for the day, allowing me to coast down to the motel on the outskirts of Sawtry where Jim is waiting – complete with new phone cables.

Before he leaves, we decide to try the all-you-can-eat buffet at Spiceland, the Indian restaurant directly next door. The food is delicious – and much needed – but the atmosphere is very different to the cosy, low-ceilinged vibe I'm used to at the average high-street curry house. Architecturally, something's awry but I can't put my finger on it. Only much later do I realise that we were eating our chicken bhunas in a converted Little Chef. The café was abandoned when an A1 upgrade left it marooned on this side road. Like many a Great North Road building over many a century, it's had to adapt to changing times.

DAY THREE

SAWTRY TO SOUTH WITHAM

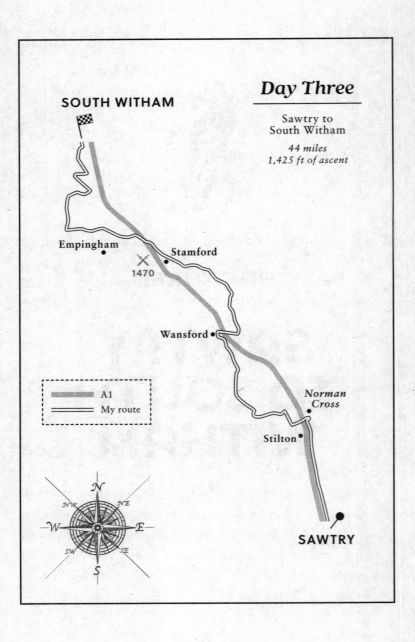

SOUTH WITHAM

Day Three

Sawtry to
South Witham

*44 miles
1,425 ft of ascent*

Empingham

✕
1470

Stamford

Wansford

*Norman
Cross*

Stilton

A1
My route

SAWTRY

N
NW · NE
W · E
SW · SE
S

Redwings Lodge is cheap and cheerful, with the emphasis on the cheerful. All of the staff have smiles on their faces as we politely tiptoe around each other in the rather cramped breakfast room – basically last night's bar with cereal boxes. Around 50 Chinese tourists are in residence, meaning I must weave my bike through a traffic jam of trolley cases as we all try to check out. I attempt a bit of sign language banter by comparing my small pannier with one lady's large suitcase. But it's so lost in translation that I end up taking hers outside, having seemingly been mistaken for a Lycra-clad bell boy.

The BBC weather forecaster had decreed that the north would be warm and sunny, the south cold and grey. I'm delighted to discover that today the north begins in Sawtry. My road continues in the same straight and fast vein as yesterday, but because the sun is shining I see it through different eyes. My shadow appears directly in front of me, orange tip butterflies are on the wing, even the chiffchaffs have more squeak in their song.

But I see nothing of the village. Indeed as far as the Great North Road is concerned, Sawtry has simply disappeared. While its centre had always been to the west, it used to spread this far. If I'd been cycling here 100 years ago, I would have been spoiled for choice; there was the Rest-a-Wyle café, The Royal Oak pub and two garages. Exploring online the previous evening, I'd found a beautiful black and white photograph showing a car being towed back to base after an early GNR prang. But now, with the traffic speeding by at 70 mph, there is no money to be made from travellers – and Sawtry has retreated in response. The solitary reminder of the old days is a church graveyard – without a church. St Andrew's was demolished in about 1880, all that survives is a mix of disorderly old gravestones and some better-behaved new ones. I root around under the trees and find a damaged slab of slate, dedicated to the memory of the Leicestershire man James Ratford, apparently killed by his best friend in a duel on 25 June 1756. Why, we simply don't know.

———

I adjust to life in the saddle – it's starting to become second nature – and take stock of the landscape. The author Chris Cooper talks about settlements becoming sparser to the north of Alconbury and the point is well made. The wind coming in from the north east has whipped across flat field after flat field, with only the distant spire of Whittlesey church to indicate any habitation. Clearly the A1 divides Cambridgeshire simply by its presence. But it also marks an invisible boundary between a hillier west and a flatter east. A look at the map shows that the latter is parcelled up into rectangles defined by artificial waterways. A word cloud of place names here would see "fen", "drain", "cut" and "mere" writ large.

In fact the modern road is in particularly imposing form. Three and sometimes four lanes of ultra-smooth carriageway were installed each way around the beginning of the 2000s. I remember it well because I was the local TV reporter at the time. The delays were endless. At one point an effigy dressed in a Peterborough United shirt was hung from a tall post at Sawtry, perhaps in protest. On a slow news day, I dubbed it "The Angel of the East" and somehow managed to get a two-minute item past the news editor.

These days the road builders don't slam through villages. They prefer to slalom gently around them. Sawtry on one side and a former coaching inn called The Crown and Woolpack surviving as a farm on the other. The village of Stilton is also swerved, reducing the southern end of its high street to a dead end. It means a detour (indeed a detour involving me cycling south which never feels right) but in this case it's eminently worthwhile because Stilton presents the perfect vista of the highway in coaching times – broad, pub-lined and quietly dignified. Not for nothing did the writer W. Outram Tristram, in his 1893 book *Coaching*

Days and Coaching Ways, describe it here as "the artery of a nation".

Funnily enough it should also have been home to the country's first turnpike – what we would now call a toll road. As long ago as 1663 a long stretch of road from Wadesmill in Hertfordshire to Stilton was earmarked for the experiment. Turnpike roads were barred by a long pole (or pike) that could be lifted (or turned) upon payment. In Stilton, the idea proved so controversial that they didn't even build the apparatus. But over the next 100 years the idea would catch on and ultimately lead to a massive improvement in the country's communication network. Before the age of the turnpike, roads were shockingly bad. Even a major thoroughfare like the Great North Road was likely to be almost impassable in bad weather and deeply rutted in good. Turnpikes transferred the costs of maintenance from local people – who often didn't go near them – to the road users themselves. And while they were not always popular, no one could deny that they worked. In that respect an improved network of coach services spurred on the creation of further pay-per-drive roads – and vice-versa.

Stilton finally got a working turnpike in about 1710. The increase in traffic soon resulted in an increase in trade at The Bell – a fine coaching inn on the high street, built of solid limestone and weighty wooden beams. It's too early for The Bell to be open today, but I'd visited it shortly beforehand on a research recce. The best seat in the house is within the bay window, protruding onto the road itself. I remember four hand-pulled pumps directly facing me at the bar, a discreet violin concerto purring away in the background and the cheesiest chalkboard ever.

"Sweet dreams are made of this," it ran. "Who am I to diss a Brie. I Cheddar the world and the Feta Cheese, everybody's looking for Stilton."

You do have to try the Stilton. But the controversial question in these parts is does the cheese come from the village? All the old books say it was made in Leicestershire, with Stilton simply being the shop window because of its prominent position on the Great North Road.

On this, Harper couldn't have been clearer:

Stilton cheese is not, nor ever was, made at Stilton, or anywhere near it. It originated with Mrs Paulet of Wymondham near Melton Mowbray, who first supplied it to Cooper Thornhill, the once celebrated landlord of The Bell for the use of the table provided for the coach passengers and other travellers who dined there.

As Harper points out, the response was positive.

Mrs Paulet's cheeses immediately struck connoisseurs as a revelation, and they came into demand, not only on Thornhill's table, but were eagerly purchased for themselves or friends by those who travelled this way.

"We are now happy to correct that version of history," begins the revisionist view on the pub's website. Cheese-making, argue the locals, had undoubtedly flourished here since the eighteenth century. I'm not convinced by the History of Stilton 2.0, but either way my blue-veined classic arrived at a perfect room temperature, complete with dark plum bread and onion chutney. Taken with a pint, it was delicious.

The fortunes of The Bell have always waxed and waned with the popularity of the road. The coaching era was its heyday, with 300 horses stabled here and an equal number at The Angel opposite. But when the railway bypassed Stilton, what we would now call "footfall" plummeted, so much so that it was downgraded from a town to a village in 1894. The Bell declined too. The five-year restoration project which produced the friendly inn we see today was completed as recently as 1990. I particularly love the sign – a massive image of a red and yellow bell, hanging over the pavement below and kept secure by a complicated panoply of wrought iron. If you turned it horizontally and gave it some legs, I'm sure six people could sit round it for a pint. Within the pub, the central coaching archway survives but is now encased within glass doors and windows. From the courtyard travellers can read the mileages etched into the voussoir stones. London is 74 miles to the south, Stamford a further 14 miles north.

Today, my final task in Stilton is to take a short detour to the churchyard. The most famous grave belongs to Cooper

Thornhill. But I prefer the headstone to Thomas Lunn who died about a century later on 6 June 1856.

"He was night coachman thirty years on the Great North Road," runs the inscription.

Thirty years! Thirty cold winters swaddled in greatcoat upon greatcoat. Hundreds of nights needing some sort of instinctive infrared vision to spot every pot hole in every unpaved road. Every night, *their* lives in your hands. The powers of concentration, the speed of thought, the dexterity of reins. Quite a job for quite a period.

———

I head north, meeting the A1 at Norman Cross. These days the place name refers to little more than a roundabout, but once it had a sort of fame as the home of the world's first purpose-built prisoner of war (POW) camp. An elevated junction takes me across the traffic toward a discreet cul-de-sac which is home to a scattering of houses, a low-rise hotel and a very striking monument to the men who died here during the Napoleonic Wars.

At that time Britain used to house its foreign POWs on the south coast in crumbling forts and decommissioned ships. But the scale of the conflict meant they needed to get more organised. Over the winter of 1796–1797 a team of carpenters built a pre-fab jail from scratch. This so-called Prison Depot could house 7,000 men. A cannon mounted on a central tower deterred escape attempts from within, while two regiments of British soldiers patrolled the perimeter. Peterborough Museum – just a few miles down the road – recreates one of these "barrack blocks" – complete with wooden beams, back-breakingly low ceilings, even the sounds of prisoners snoring. The curators have also gathered an impressively large collection of artefacts made by the inmates themselves. There are intricate working models of guillotines, a Noah's ark and lots of smaller items like fans and vanity cases which were sold to local people. Made from bone, paper or straw they bear testament to endless hours of captivity.

More than 1,700 prisoners died here between 1797 and 1814 – many during an outbreak of typhoid. The monument – a pillar topped by a bronze eagle – was erected 100 years later at a time when the countries were brothers in arms on the fields of Flanders. There have been some ups and downs since. The original bronze was stolen in 1990 and the column had to be moved a few years later when the A1 was upgraded. But in 2005 a new eagle was unveiled, with the Duke of Wellington doing the honours. Incredibly, more than 1,000 people turned up for the ceremony – clearly the memory still resonates.

———

The A1 has been following Ermine Street in these parts, but north of Norman Cross it drifts absent-mindedly north west, seemingly unwilling to cross the River Nene. Drivers can stop at The Sibson Inn, once a pub, then converted to a farmhouse and now returned to its original function. Alongside its barn, a stone marks the 81st mile from London. But it's actually more than a milestone; it's a horseman's upping block. Inscribed "EB 1703", it's a rare survivor of a series installed by the merchant Edmund Boulter to help him travel between large estates in Cambridgeshire and Yorkshire.

An early nineteenth-century gazetteer entitled *A New and Accurate Description of all Direct and Principle Cross Roads of England and Wales* explains:

"From Stilton to Grantham, at convenient distances, are stones with three steps, placed there by a Mr Boulter, for the easy mounting of his horse, he being a very corpulent man and travelled this road every week for many years…"

There's no easy way for a cyclist to follow Boulter's route toward Peterborough and Stamford, so I re-cross the motorway and plunge westwards into a noticeably different landscape: rounded hills, smaller fields, more fragrant hedgerows even. It's more evidence that the A1 route divides Cambridgeshire into a hilly west and a fenny east. I take a sharp right into the village of Folksworth and then an equally sharp left through tiny Morborne before I realise that I'm starting to run on empty. I simply haven't eaten enough at my budget breakfast. I limp on until Elton where, thankfully, there's a village shop selling squares of home-made flapjack. I don't just eat them, I devour them in the manner of a dog – but feel satisfyingly more human about ten minutes later. I'm discovering that "hungry" and "bike-hungry" are entirely different things.

Elton appears to have a strict dress code for all of its houses. Some unwritten law suggests they must be built of sandy-coloured bricks of coursed limestone, with dressed limestone for the fancy bits and Collyweston slate for the roofs. Each looks reassuringly ancient and sturdy. It's only later that I realise I've entered England's limestone belt – a diagonal sash of calcium carbonate which runs under the country from Yorkshire to Dorset. Elton is the first of a series of honey-coloured villages which will continue until the outskirts of Grantham.

The countryside continues to impress as I make my way along a ridge road. I lean back, stretch my aching muscles and risk a few yards no-handed. The bike has drop handlebars, but I'm mostly riding in a more relaxed position – with my hands on the hoods rather than the drops, as the jargon has it. The sun's rays are getting warmer and the skylarks and yellowhammers make their presence heard; it feels like we've all got our May back. It's becoming clear that it's taken two days to leave the heavily populated south of the country behind. I'm not sure I've made it to the Midlands, but it certainly now feels like Middle England. To my left there are fine views down to the River Nene – which meanders to meet my road at Wansford, another limestone village which feels as if it should be populated by Victorian extras from a Sunday night period drama. The old Great North Road came in from the right here to use the ancient bridge. I'm not aware of quite how close the modern A1 is until I turn a corner into a short surviving stretch of London Road, where I see the green and red livery of an Eddie Stobart lorry steaming past.

I should be getting used to this; after all the very purpose of the ride is to shadow the modern A1 as closely as I can. But every time, the furious insistence of engine noise jolts me from one existence to another. A fast dual carriageway is a world unto itself in a way that the slower Great North Road never had to be.

The Haycock Hotel – all sash windows and tall chimneys – still dominates this strategic corner. It's a huge site and a useful reminder of how much land the old coaching inns needed to ply their trade. The hotel for the guests wasn't the half of it; stabling and the ancillary trades took up even more space. In sleepy old Wansford those buildings survive and are now turned over for small businesses and bed and breakfast accommodation. The hotel trades on a seventeenth-century piece of doggerel concerning an intoxicated rustic peddlar called Barnaby, who falls asleep on top of a bale of hay that gets swept away on a flooded River Nene:

On a haycock sleeping soundly
Th'river rose and tooke me roundly
Down the current, people cryed

Sleeping, down the stream I hyed
"Where away," quoth they, "from Greenland?"
"No, from Wansford Brigs in England."

I first find "Drunken Barnaby" on the battered old pub sign, but later realise that other languorous images of him – complete with pitchfork, hat and neckerchief – are to be seen everywhere.

From The Haycock I cross Wansford's long bridge with its angular cutwaters. In the central refuge a boundary stone tells me I'm crossing from Huntingdonshire into the Soke of Peterborough. Sokes – as administrative or judicial areas – go back to the Norman Conquest. This particular one clung on as a semi-autonomous part of Northamptonshire until 1974. Huntingdonshire was relegated to district council status at the same time. Both now form part of a larger Cambridgeshire.

It's a truly idyllic spot and I am unable to resist a wooden seat situated invitingly at a staggered crossroads just beyond – especially as the hill ahead looks mildly taxing. It's almost become a reflex reaction to reach for Harper on these occasions, but I'm surprised to find him offering a very different perspective:

Now that there is no longer a turnpike gate at this point
to bring the traffic to a slow pace, this descent is fruitful
in accidents... at least one cyclist has been killed here in an

attempt to negotiate this sharp curve on the descent into the cross-road. An inoffensive cottage standing at the corner... has received many a cyclist through its window.

I try to work out which house that might have been – without success. I then crest the hill, re-cross the A1 and escape onto a back road toward Stamford via Southorpe and Barnack. I was vaguely aware of Barnack as a place where limestone was quarried. I hadn't realised that it was worked out as long ago as 1500, having provided much of the raw materials for both Peterborough and Ely cathedrals. Today the site of the quarry is known as the Hills and Holes – as good a description as any of the lunar lumps and bumps that have lain largely undisturbed for half a millennium.

From Barnack I soon pick up the boundary wall for the massive Burleigh estate, home to the famous horse trials – a sort of Wimbledon for three-day eventing. Then it's glorious Stamford with its history, its river and its limestone buildings. My road brings me into the town close to The George, another coaching inn vying for superlatives. The George isn't exactly shy. It announces itself with a wooden beam slung across the width of the Great North Road – as if it owns the place. It stands "as a gesture of welcome to the honest traveller and of warning to the highwayman" according to the pub's literature. Given that there may have been an inn here for 1,000 years, it would be a brave health and safety official who would take it down now.

The George has always been used by the great and the good, including Kings Charles I and William III as well as a victorious Duke of Cumberland returning from the Battle of Culloden. Enter via the high street and the visitor is still greeted by the London Room to the left and the York Bar to the right. I feel instantly at home whichever direction I am heading. While The Haycock felt self-consciously restored, The George feels as if it's just kept on going through the centuries.

I take another photo. If I had to sum up the Great North Road in one single image it would be here – the old road heading down to the Welland and then, timelessly, straight up into the heart of the town. The foreground framed by the wooden sign; the high ground dominated by the magnificent tower and steeple of St Mary's Church. I then say goodbye to Stamford Baron – the part which lies to the south of the river and used to be in Northamptonshire – and get agreeably lost in Lincolnshire's Stamford Town. There aren't that many streets, but the succession of churches – St Mary's, St Martin's, St Michael the Greater, St George's, All Saints and St John's – as well as a succession of artful corners and pedestrian squares always leave me embarrassingly flummoxed. (In my defence I'd like to blame tenth-century Danes. The Great North Road had to bypass their ancient burh – or borough – in the middle of the town and the resulting dog-leg in the road remains a pain for traffic to this day.) Geographically, Stamford was spoiled for choice when it came to local limestone quarries. Architecturally, it shows. For my money it is one of the most beautiful towns in England. The pedestrianised high street forces me to get off the bike and walk – as ever in the hope of a decent café. And at this slower pace I can appreciate the quality of the stonework in everything from the building housing WHSmith to the Georgian Gothic of St Michael's.

One coffee and two requests for directions later, I'm heading up Scotgate on the Great Casterton road where a milestone tells me I'm 90 miles from London. There's no sign, but somewhere along this road I leave Lincolnshire for the tiny county of Rutland. Then it's back to the A1. I'd hoped I might be able to find a pavement here, much as I had done in Bedfordshire, but the road has become a different beast, so again I will need to plough west toward Empingham.

By my reckoning at least 25 battles have been fought within two or three miles of the Great North Road. But the Battle of Empingham is one of only two to have actually been fought up and down it. Admittedly it's no Hastings, but nevertheless many thousands probably died here on 12 March 1470. It was fought between Edward IV and a group of Lincolnshire rebels led by the nobleman Sir Robert Welles. The king had marched his forces up from London, reaching Stamford by the day of the battle. That morning his scouts unexpectedly spotted their quarry, prompting the rebels to line up directly across the Great North Road at Tickencote.

Both sides could soon see each other across the gentle slope. Edward was with Welles's father and the father of another rebel leader, effectively holding them hostage. Now, before battle was joined, the older men were brought out in front of the troops. It was time to exact symbolic and bloody revenge. Their sons, watching from afar, had been warned.

"A burly retainer stepped forward and did the deed," wrote Rupert Matthews in his 2013 book *The Battle of Losecoat Field*, seemingly the only author to have considered the battle worthy of its own book.

"The severed heads of the two men were picked up by their hair and displayed first to Edward's army and then to the rebels."

The battle itself seems to have been relatively straightforward by the standards of the time. Edward's men were outnumbered but they had the firepower, the discipline and the tactical nous. They pushed up the Great North Road, routing the left wing of the rebel army. Soon the entire contingent was being chased north, with nobles being killed or captured, but commoners largely pardoned. The conflict is also known as the The Battle of Losecoat Field – perhaps because the rebels were quick to shed the coats that showed their allegiance. A more likely explanation is so banal as to be almost comical. The site was probably named after a nearby pigsty cottage, known at the time as a "hlose-cot". Not quite so glamorous.

I love to look over the landscape of an ancient battle and try to imagine the sights and the sounds. That's all but impossible in the middle of a dual carriageway and there's certainly no interpretation board. But whether by luck or historical judgement, the engineers have built a tunnel under the A1 at this precise spot, allowing me to explore both Tickencote Warren and a copse immediately to the west. The latter, I'm delighted to discover, is still known as Bloody Oaks – history in a name, hanging by a single thread on a map. I can't find a footpath – nor as much as an oak leaf come to that – but it remains the sort of thick woodland where one can imagine a deadly game of hide and seek taking place.

Back on the bike, I never actually see the village of Empingham, striking out for first Exton and then Greetham. The sun has long gone and after 43 miles my legs are going too. But tonight I'm not staying in a hotel. Helpfully, my brother-in-law and sister-in-law live just minutes from the Great North Road in the next village. So at half past five, I sink first into a bath and then a sofa at South Witham. My kit goes into the washing machine and there's wining, dining and good conversation. Unexpectedly, it feels quite strange to be re-inserted into normal life. Clearly after just three days I already belong to the road.

DAY FOUR

SOUTH WITHAM TO AUSTERFIELD

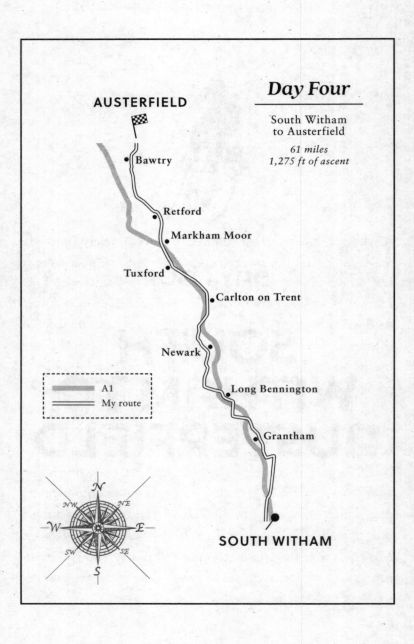

Day Four

South Witham
to Austerfield

61 miles
1,275 ft of ascent

AUSTERFIELD

Bawtry

Retford

Markham Moor

Tuxford

Carlton on Trent

Newark

Long Bennington

Grantham

A1
My route

SOUTH WITHAM

Brother-in-law Dave hadn't been massively into the details of the ride last night, but now he's all over it. Ordnance Survey maps engulf the kitchen table and the Harley Davidson is growling in the garage. He's got stuff to do this morning but promises to follow me up later in the day. I transfer everything heavy from my pannier to his before he can change his mind. I have more than 60 miles to cover today, so every little helps.

I'm travelling light. For life on two wheels I have one jacket, three base layers, one pair of shorts and one pair of full-length trousers. For my minimal life off the bike, there's a pair of trainers, another pair of shorts, one t-shirt and a basic wash bag. So far it's been much colder than I had anticipated and I'm already regretting not packing a pair of jeans. I've acquired more underwear, energy gels and Midlands maps from a package delivered to South Witham in advance; a northern version is on its way to my planned stop-off in Newcastle.

But back to the road. The A1 gradually straightens itself out after Stamford so that by South Witham it's heading due north. This stretch of tarmac holds the collective memories of both the Roman-era Ermine Street and the more modern Great North Road. It's a shame there isn't some sort of cycle path because it still has the wild and woolly feel of the old days, despite being a dual carriageway. There are also three ancient inns surviving in various states of repair. In the second half of the twentieth century The Ram Jam was probably the most famous. A lovely looking pub of limestone yellow, it now lies boarded up next to a petrol station on the northbound carriageway. The Ram Jam was never a coaching inn, but that doesn't mean that coaches didn't stop there. Certainly unauthorised stops were a major headache for Post Office boss Thomas Hasker in 1800, as noted by Frederick Wilkinson in his 2007 book *Royal Mail Coaches – An Illustrated History*. "Stopping at ale houses on the road between stage and stage under pretence of watering horses, but in reality to drink, have been found very detrimental to the service," Hasker proclaimed in a nineteenth-century version of the all-staff email. He promised to "annihilate so shameful a practice". But on a cold winter's night with the lights of The Ram Jam shining brightly, who knows what really happened?

How did the pub get its name? According to one story, Ram Jam was an Indian liqueur – the recipe for which was brought back to England by an old colonial. But another theory, backed up by the battered pub sign, talks of a trickster convincing a gullible landlord that he could draw mild and bitter from one barrel by "ramming" his left thumb in the hole of the first barrel while "jamming" his right in the second. With the innkeeper stuck, the cheeky rascal was free to seduce his wife or run off without paying the bill, depending on who was telling the story.

As a student in the 1980s, I travelled this road regularly. There weren't that many Southerners hacking their way up to Newcastle University, so we'd share lifts where possible. Lunch was normally at The Ram Jam, not necessarily because it was any good, but simply because we loved the name. We weren't the only ones to be inspired. The American soul singer Geno Washington named his backing group The Ram Jam Band in its honour. With such a reputation, it happily survived until well into this century. But now it seems to be almost impossible for an old-fashioned pub to survive on a fast highway. As a result you do fear for the building's very future.

The other two pubs on this stretch had fallen foul of changing fashions many decades earlier. Both The New Inn at Greetham and The Black Bull at North Witham were reliant on the coaching trade and had been converted into farmhouses by the time Harper came calling. These days the New Inn complex is split into two houses, well-screened behind the northbound carriageway. The Black Bull, on the southbound side, has come full circle. While the pub itself was knocked down many decades ago, the accommodation building was re-opened as the Black Bull A1 Lodge in 2016.

From Dave and Sue's house I take a B-road which skirts the edge of neighbouring North Witham along roads which never seem to be flat. It's 21 miles between Stamford and Grantham, according to Harper it was an article of faith amongst cyclists that the stretch contained 21 hills too.

The shortest of detours takes me to the hamlet of Woolsthorpe, where I find a smart seventeenth-century farmhouse with an ancient apple tree in its grounds. It's an arthritic-looking specimen whose main trunk only extends skywards with the help of a couple of crutches. But this house is the birthplace of the scientist Sir Isaac Newton and this tree has become a place of pilgrimage – it's the one which helped to inspire his famous universal law of gravitation.

In his 1752 book *Sir Isaac Newton's Life*, William Stukeley – Newton's first biographer – takes up the story:

"The notion of gravitation came into his mind. 'Why should that apple always descend perpendicularly to the ground? Why should it not go sideways or upwards? But constantly to the earth's centre? Assuredly, the reason is that the earth draws it.'"

Newton's friend Alexander Pope put it more pithily:

"Nature and Nature's laws lay hid in night. God said, Let Newton be and all was light."

I like Woolsthorpe. It's less manicured than the average National Trust property – less pot pourri, more drafty fireplaces and mud on your shoes. I shuffle round the farmhouse on a guided tour with a mixture of interested locals and international tourists. Newton says he did the greatest work of his long career here between 1665 and 1666. Our National Trust guide isn't too hot on her science, but she loves the personal stories behind the great man. Newton was only at Woolsthorpe Manor because of an outbreak of plague at Cambridge University. During his own coronavirus-style lockdown, he had unexpected time to study and think. The guide takes great delight in telling us how he had the classic "mad scientist" tics. The bed was never made, the chamber pot was always full, meals would go uneaten and stray scientific papers would be strewn everywhere. Us visitors listen carefully and respectfully. This is, after all, the man who invented calculus and had three laws of motion named after him.

After the tour we all make a beeline for that decrepit tree.

"I just want to touch the leaves to get a bit of genius," jokes one dad to his children.

He's not alone. People come to see it from all over the world. And "descendants" of the tree have been planted everywhere from Trinity College, Cambridge to the Massachusetts Institute of Technology in the USA and Tianjin University in China.

From Woolsthorpe my route takes me across to Colsterworth where the Great North Road and Ermine

Street go their separate ways. The ever-pragmatic GNR starts to head north west, while Ermine Street will continue due north as far as the Humber. And I do mean due north; the Roman road runs as straight as a die. They call Ermine Street "High Dike" in these parts – although I don't get my intonation right until I ask for directions. I had it down as "High DIKE", but it turns out it's "'IGH dike". As I follow the road for a few miles I get one last blast of the Fens – a smell of diced carrots wafting across from a giant processing factory. I then duck left into a handy valley. Alert to the imminence of a north/south moment I now feel as if I am hurtling through an obscure corner of the Yorkshire Dales – hills tumbling down on both sides to my narrow lane. There's barely a hedge, not a single farmhouse, just the odd stone trough to indicate human involvement. I haven't been able to reach this speed for ages and I feel my cheeks smarten against the wind as I freewheel down to Little Ponton without a care in the world.

Then it's Grantham – which underwhelms me. After 24 hours in the beautiful limestone belt, I suppose any return to red brick was going to be tough. St Wulfram's tall church tower adds some grandeur, but that's about it. The shops look thoroughly average, the roads are congested and I find no coffee shop that looks half as promising as the one in Biggleswade. As a result I open my book on a park bench rather than a café table. But once again Mr Harper and I are in perfect harmony:

The expectant traveller comes to Grantham hopeful of a fine old town with streets and buildings befitting its historic dignity; but these hopes are soon dispelled by grimy engine-rooms and roads gritty with coal-dust...

And then he really sticks the boot in:

Grantham is a red-brick town, and modern red brick at that. A cruelly vulgar Town Hall, all variegated brick, iron crestings, and general spikiness, fondly believed to be 'Italian' testifies at once to the expansive prosperity of Grantham and to its artlessness.

It's worth saying at this point that Harper was a confirmed Southerner. From about Grantham onwards, one feels as if he's out of his comfort zone.

Historically, the town claims a famous son and a famous daughter – separated by 300 years. The son is Sir Isaac Newton – on the grounds that he went to school in the town. Grantham loves Newton. A pub and a shopping centre are named after him and there's a grand statue too. Our man stands, robed and magisterial, holding a scroll and looking like an Old Testament prophet.

The famous daughter is the former Conservative Prime Minister Margaret Thatcher. She was born in 1925 in a flat above her father's grocer's shop – directly on the Great North Road. In the early pages of her autobiography we see

Grantham through the prism of her parents' Methodism and her own prodigious appetite for education. Her father was a huge inspiration. As well as running the grocery business Alfred Roberts was a councillor, magistrate, school governor and lay preacher. The sermons the young Margaret Roberts heard and the passionate discussions she had with other (mostly Left-leaning) Methodists stood her in good stead for her later political career. She won a scholarship to Kesteven and Grantham Girls' School, which in turn prepared her for Oxford. When she was ennobled in 1992 she chose to become Baroness Thatcher of Kesteven – rather than of Grantham – a tribute to the school to which she owed so much.

Thatcher is much less visible in the town than Newton. But in 2017 an improved display was installed within Grantham Museum. While it's clearly been put together on a limited budget (both Alfred and Margaret would surely have approved) it does an impressive job of explaining how Grantham moulded her and how she moulded late twentieth-century Britain. Some American visitors, I was told, virtually worship at the prize exhibit – her bed. You might have thought that a handbag, a hockey stick or indeed the unforgettable *Spitting Image* puppet would have proved more popular, but no, it's a wooden bed frame with a stripy blue mattress that gets them going. The curators have also had the brilliantly simple idea of installing a small sitting room à la 1979 – the year she became Prime Minister. The sofa looks frighteningly similar to the one I grew up with although the manifestoes of the three main political parties never made it to our coffee table. For added authenticity, her Labour predecessor Jim Callaghan is on loop on the TV while a series of Thatcher quotes adorn the back wall. Among them: "I started life with two great advantages: no money and good parents".

Leaving the museum I look for the surviving coaching inn. And I'm sorry Grantham but I don't warm to this either. In theory the Angel and Royal is right up there in the Great North Road pantheon. It has a claim to be England's oldest pub, having started life as a hostelry for the Knights Templar as early as 1203. Over the centuries kings and queens have stayed here – they even claim that Richard III signed the Duke of Buckingham's death warrant within its walls. So there's no shortage of history. But my first problem was finding it. It's quite a modestly sized building on an otherwise anonymous stretch of the high street. Good coaching inns dominate their town centres, this one doesn't. I step inside to an empty reception room with no one at the desk and little sign of life. I mooch around the narrow yard with its converted stable blocks and try again; still no one. My coffee would have to wait. Clearly the Angel has an impressive pedigree, but I found no evidence of the bustle that surely defines a good inn, whatever the century.

Thirsty and uncaffeinated, I get back on the bike to discover that Grantham offers its best side to the north. Alfred Roberts's old shop is at the corner of North

Parade and Broad Street. These days it's a health centre – appropriately named Living Health, it's the kind of place where you might go for reflexology or acupuncture. The bread oven survives behind the counter and there's an original fireplace too, although above it you'll find a TV screen offering soothing advertisements for products like a Nourishing Sea Mud Therapy Wrap. Over the years the manager has grown used to people standing outside, reading the small plaque and perhaps taking a few photos.

"Some of them do stand there for quite a long while," she tells me.

"Does it feel like being in a goldfish bowl?"

"Well a bit, but we always wave at them."

The Roberts family owned No 2 – the corner shop on a terraced row. Living Health has expanded to include No 4 and No 6 too, with a variety of treatment rooms on three floors.

"Would you like a tour?" she asks.

Silly question. She takes me up two flights of steep stairs to see the Blessed Margaret's bedroom. It's the smallest of the treatment rooms, perhaps 10 feet by 12 feet with windows on both sides, peering out over the Great North Road traffic. The bed the Americans admire so much, once belonged here. Back down at reception I ask the manager about the politics of it all. There's a collective sucking of teeth and furrowing of brows from everyone within earshot, including customers. People, I discover, Have Views. But in this line of work there's already a blanket ban on such talk. And when your business just happens to be based at the former home of Mrs T, that's a very handy rule to hang on to.

From North Parade, it's a steady climb passing Victorian villas to the village of Great Gonerby. There's another tall church steeple made of Ancaster stone – they're very good at those around here – but it's the clock face that grabs the attention. The people of Great Gonerby are proud to be known as "clockpelters". In other words they threw (or maybe they still throw?) things at the church clock. Was it some sort of rite of passage for youngsters? There are other theories, but the village sign shows five urchins chucking great clods clock-wards. In addition the village has recently unveiled a wooden statue where the pond once stood – and the mud was once gleaned. In polished elm, it shows a boy in mid-throw – half Just William, half "Freddie" Flintoff. Delightful.

Great Gonerby lies at the summit of a 370-foot-high hill, a hill the coachmen hated and novelists – including Sir Walter Scott – exaggerated. Since their time it's been softened slightly by a cutting into its northern side, but cyclists still build up quite a speed heading down, the gradient all the more impressive for the views of the Vale of Belvoir beyond. The old road rejoins the A1 at the bottom of the hill, where there's an out-of-town shopping centre called Downtown. And Downtown is where I have a quiet meltdown at a particularly unprepossessing café within a mini-service station.

On the approach, I'm suddenly aware that I can't pedal. I can't physically push one leg down after the other. My hands shake on the handlebars and I quickly scramble off the bike for fear of falling off instead. So what on earth is going on? Rational thought arrives, but only with difficulty. Like yesterday I'd had a late start. Like yesterday I probably hadn't eaten enough breakfast. On that occasion Elton's emergency flapjack had saved the day. This time it's too late. This time my body has gone on strike in protest.

In cyclists' lingo I had "bonked". I had completely run out of gas. I'd read about the phenomenon, but never experienced it.

It's a doubly annoying sensation. First, because you feel ill. Second, because you have a light-bulb realisation that you haven't looked after yourself properly in the first place. If you were only able to co-ordinate your limbs, you'd kick yourself for your own stupidity.

I am no kind of athlete, I just like riding a bike. True, I had recently completed my first 100-mile-in-a-day ride around Norfolk, but it turns out that doesn't give you immunity against a lack of common sense a few months later. An average of 50 miles a day over 11 days is requiring proper preparation. To be in peak condition, this very un-peaky 50-something is slowly discovering that he needs to have a solid breakfast by 7.30 a.m., be on the road by 8.30 a.m. and take a caffeine hit by 10 a.m. Regular small amounts of refuelling work best after that, followed by a proper meal in the evening.

But I am still very much at the trial and error stage. Which is why I am sitting in Costa Coffee, getting the shakes and doubting my ability to make it to the end of the day, let alone the end of the country. I drink cappuccino and eat chocolate. Decision-making becomes easier once I've refuelled. I'm not going to end up in the back of a Lincolnshire ambulance, I tell myself. At the very least it will be a Nottinghamshire ambulance.

From Downtown I cross the A1 and tack north and west, a tad shakily. I'm now in the middle of the vast patchwork of fields I could see from the Great Gonerby summit. These flat roads all feel the same before I survive a slightly hairy re-crossing of the A1 at Foston – four lanes of 70 mph traffic without the benefit of a bridge. Foston is followed by the well-named Long Bennington with its never-ending main street.

Looking at the map, I'd imagined a straggling and struggling high street with a convenience store if I was lucky. Perhaps ten years ago that would have been accurate, but no longer. The village I cycle through comes complete with obviously thriving pubs and the SixtyTwo café overflowing with club cyclists. Having only just refuelled at Downtown I keep cycling. Reader, don't make the same mistake. Ignore the Grantham Moto and settle in here. Established in a former hairdresser's shop in 2012, SixtyTwo has been surfing the wave of new money pouring into the village in recent years, buoyed by a relatively easy Grantham to London rail commute. Cyclist-wise, Long Bennington is a decent distance from places like Nottingham and Lincoln so there's no surprise that it's popular. They even have blankets for the outside tables. I quite like the thought of super-fit cyclists quietly succumbing to soft temptation as a northerly whips down the high street.

————

From Long Bennington there are more windswept fields before I'm blessed with a stroke of luck – a lost railway line with a new role as a cycle path. Suddenly I am heading toward Newark, traffic-free and wind-free with just a few tree root tentacles to negotiate in compensation. True, I am drifting rather to the west of the Great North Road but Route 64 offers a warts-and-all look at the massive gypsum factories that Newark is famous for – Jericho Quarry to my right and Hawton Works to the left. Gypsum is what you need to make plaster – everything from materials for the building trade to the casts used by hospitals. Digging the stuff out of the ground has been part of Newark's economy since at least Roman times. Certainly the mapmaker John Speed reported that the folk of Nottinghamshire knew all about it in the seventeenth century. In his 1606 book *Theatre of the Empire of Great Britain*, he wrote:

"Therein groweth a Stone softer then Alabaster, but being burned maketh a plaister harder than that of Paris, wherewith they floor their upper Rooms; for betwixt the joysts they lay only long Bulrushes, and thereon spread this Plaister, which being thoroughly dry becomes most solid and hard, so that it seemeth rather to be firm stone than mortar, and is trod upon without all danger."

My railway path continues to Newark station, but I come up for air on the fiercely red-brick Barnby Road. That's the other great advantage of a cycle path, you bypass the "could-be-anywhere" fringe and emerge when a town really starts to look like itself.

Historically Newark was known as "the key to the north" – and now that phrase feels good. As though I am getting somewhere. The tall spire of St Mary Magdalene guides me to the market place at the end of a busy morning. The red and white canopies of the stalls rustle gently in the breeze as the traders pack up, shouting friendly insults to each other. It's just about warm enough to sit outside at The Green Olive Café and admire the view. East Midlands towns believe in central market places and few do them better than Newark. Give me a narrow high street and my eye never naturally rises higher than the modern shop fronts. Give me a market square and every storey from every century comes under close inspection. Do architects raise their game as a result or is it just that I'm paying more attention? Either way, I enjoy a solid meal in scenic surroundings, satisfied that I've got 30 miles under my belt.

If you wander round this town, it doesn't take long to discover that one particular period of history looms large. The English Civil War put Newark on the front line. It had always been a strategic place – take Newark Castle, they said, and you could hold sway over the Great North Road, the River Trent and the Fosse Way heading up to Lincoln. So in 1642 this staunchly Royalist town found itself close to the Parliamentarian strongholds in the south and east. As a result it was besieged three times. On the first two occasions it saw off its attackers – although they needed the help of a rampaging Prince Rupert for the second one. The third siege was the longest – a desperate six-month period when the population resorted to killing horses and dogs for their meat. This time they did surrender, but only on the specific orders of Charles I. Even then, Newark's mayor had resisted, arguing that the town should instead "Trust in God and Sally Forth". That phrase has since become the town's motto. It makes me like Newark ever more.

There's evidence of the sieges if you know where to look. The hole in the church spire comes courtesy of a musket ball. The black and white timber-framed building is both a Greggs bakery and Grade I listed, but more importantly it was the Governor's House – the HQ during the sieges. Then there's the National Civil War Centre, a museum opened in 2015. Despite that "national" word, you actually get just the one room on the conflict for your money. But it's big, informative and stylish, taking you on a complete Civil War journey, right from the accession of Charles I. Of course Newark takes centre stage. I particularly enjoy the short films displayed within a tiny cinema at one end of the room. I watch three, each one a tiny vignette, but all beautifully scripted. Together they capture the insecurities, the split loyalties and the ambiguities of the time. More than any artefact they force me to wonder whose side I would have been on.

Newark is too good to rush. So I walk with the bike to explore thoroughfares with ancient names like Slaughterhouse Lane and Lombard Street before finding my way to the remains of Newark Castle overlooking the Trent. Seeing the bridge, I decide that my Downtown wobble is behind me. It's time to trust in God and sally forth – not least because this bridge means I'm back on the Great North Road. I cross one branch of the Trent here and another a mile later at South Muskham. The low-lying area in between used to be bedevilled by flooding; it wasn't until the eighteenth century that the civil engineer John Smeaton built his mile-long causeway. All these years later, Smeaton's Arches are still keeping us dry.

From here the A1 sits happily in the Trent valley, gently curving left and right to bypass the various villages that the GNR used to run straight through. At the second attempt I find a route to Cromwell from North Muskham with the help of a bike path directly alongside the A1. Cromwell is just as timeless as Tempsford and Stilton, with the farms which once sat directly alongside the old road now reduced to sleepy obscurity. Then a badly designed access road gets me to Carlton-on-Trent, where I pass a magnificent old smithy with a two-storey-high brick horseshoe built into its frontage. The inscription above the door is a reminder of the volume of trade in the old days:

> Gentlemen as you pass by upon this shoe,
> Pray cast an eye.
> If it be too strait I'll make it wider
> I'll ease the horse and please the rider.
> If lame from shoeing as they often are
> You may have them eased with
> The Greatest Care.

Houseowner Terry Cooper tells me that the big beams within the building still give it the air of a forge despite it being converted into a house in the 1960s. It remains a low-key tourist attraction – many a horse-drawn wedding party has posed outside over the years.

Cycling on, I spot a Ferry Lane off to my right. I never can resist a ferry – particularly a long-lost one and Carlton doesn't disappoint. It is, after all, Carlton-on-Trent. The casual visitor might never see it, but probe eastwards and you'll find the river in the middle of an extravagant meander as it heads toward the Humber. Semi-detached from the village, I find a series of buildings, all of a piece from the early twentieth century. Among them, a wharf building with the name "R. Teal, Trent Gravels" picked out in flint and stone. Sad to admit, I'm never happier than in a landscape of forgotten industrial archaeology. Two large girders point skywards, seemingly all that remains of a river winch. Nearby, a pair of 1920s semi-detached houses has nautically themed stained glass in the bay windows and "Trent View" picked out amid the pebble dash. Clearly proximity to both the Great River and the Great North Road once gave this village an added prosperity. The houses are still lived in, but at this precise moment they appear deserted and are certainly silent.

Frustratingly, I can't find any evidence of the old ferry or where it might have docked. The map shows a road on the other side of the river which would tie up nicely, but the only people on that side are anglers, half-hidden within their camouflaged hoods and pop-up tents. Shouting across to them feels like it will get me nowhere, particularly as they too are silent. Nevertheless, it's a spot that screams "geography". Sir Walter Scott called it "the hundred-armed Trent", while John Milton talked of 30 branches flowing "along the indented meads". Both numbers feel like a hefty exaggeration these days, but certainly the Trent is a more substantial river once all of its appendages have converged to the east of Newark. It forms a major barrier in these parts with bridges surprisingly few and far between. A chalky path strides beside it and, despite a gentle sense of eerie melancholy, I'm more than a little tempted to follow the river rather than the road.

But of course I backtrack to discover that the GNR and the A1 are now separate roads. The Great North Road – labelled as such on my map – has become the quiet B1164. The surface is good and the traffic is light in the early afternoon – just perfect for cycling. The sun comes out as I pass through Sutton, where an Edinburgh express keeps me company on the East Coast Main Line. Sutton is also "on-Trent", but it's perhaps more famous for its connections with the road – not least because it once held an annual festival in honour of the coaching trade.

"Coaches were compelled to stop in the village street," wrote Harper.

> And everyone was invited to partake of the good things spread out upon a tray covered with a beautiful damask napkin on which were attractively displayed plum-cakes, tartlets, gingerbread, exquisite home-made bread and biscuits, ale, currant and gooseberry wines, cherry brandy and sometimes spirits... Half a dozen damsels, rather shy, but courteously importunate, plied the passengers.

Wistfully, I munch a Twix alone at the roadside with considerably less ceremony.

Tuxford is the next place of any significance, a small town with a whitewashed coaching inn converted into a museum and art gallery. The old Newcastle Arms building has one outstanding exhibit for the Great North Road pilgrim – an original mail coach. Smartly painted in black and red and obviously well-maintained, it's nevertheless all but wedged into a small stall within the original stable block. Somehow I feel such a rare survivor deserves a grander resting place.

A modern coach pulls up outside, its passengers disgorged into the courtyard café. Not one of them gives "No 17 HOLYHEAD LONDON ROYAL MAIL" a second glance, but perhaps they're put off by the bloke with the bike staring at it rather too intently.

And I am staring. This piece of vehicular history manages to be both taller and smaller than I had imagined. While the compartment feels relatively pokey, the size of the wheels lifts the whole contraption substantially off the ground. I suddenly realise how high both the coachman and his "outsides" – passengers seated outside the compartment – would have been. I picture the coachman wrapped in his layers, whipping the four-in-hand along at maximum speed. Reaching across the protective barrier, I touch the scuffed surface of a front wheel. Finally, I think I understand the sense of exhilaration which might have been felt by the "outsides" as the coach hurtled along.

In the very centre of Tuxford, a picturesque signpost gives travellers four options: London, York, Lincoln… and Laxton.

I hunt out the map from the pannier to discover that Laxton is a tiny village to the south west. But a map-wielding MAMIL is enough to attract a couple of cyclists from the Retford Wheelers who happen to be passing through.

"Where are you going, mate?"

"Edinburgh."

"Edinburgh, wow! How many miles have you done today?"

"About forty."

"Oh. Right."

These guys are hard core. If you're not doing 100 miles a day you're no one. And my excuses revolving around "research" don't seem to cut the mustard either. But the fact that they seek me out for a chat is part of a bubble of Northern warmth that's been getting stronger all day. Somewhere between Stamford and Grantham, "barth" becomes "bath". Somewhere around Newark a friendliness kicks in too. Friendliness isn't really the word, but us Southerners struggle to find the right one. It's an unforced sense of normality in stopping to chat with a stranger – why wouldn't you? Something that feels weird down south, becomes reassuringly normal north of a line I've crossed today.

The temperature dips and crosswinds impede my journey up one more hill before I meet the modern A1 at an ancient junction. Markham Moor is where the Lincoln road joined the GNR, but in recent decades – if you look closely enough – it's also become a living museum to hospitality on the road. First, there's the Markham Moor Inn from the early nineteenth century. It finds itself on a backwater now as the interchange has marched west. Then there's a real hotchpotch of buildings scattered across the corners of the interchange – with architecture from every post-war decade. Over the years, Happy Eater, Little Chef and Burger King have all been represented here. In fact there were two Little Chefs, one of which has since been converted into a Chinese restaurant. The second – reborn as a slate-grey Starbucks – has given the junction its modern fame because it features a 1960s space-age roof – "hyperbolic paraboloid" is the technical term. Among local teenagers it's famous as the venue for a daring skateboard stunt – filmed by a handily-placed drone. Look it up on YouTube the next time you're filling up at one of two Shell garages or eating at either the traditional truckstop or the more modern McDonald's.

I ignore them all and continue to Retford – a mini-Newark, complete with elegant market square. The tables outside The Imperial are undoubtedly the place for a drink, not least because you get a great view of the flamboyant French-inspired town hall. Certainly it's good enough for some Hell's Angels from Rotherham. They're up for a chat too, after the bikers' standard opening gambit:

"There's something wrong with your bike, pal."

"Is there? What's up?"

"It's got no engine…"

Cue: hearty belly laughs all round.

In the old days the Great North Road passed through Sherwood Forest, well to the west of Retford. But between 1757 and 1760, the locals successfully petitioned for it to be re-routed in their direction. An Act of Parliament was passed and big money followed. The large town houses I pass near the square are a direct result. In 1777 the road was followed by a new canal, which meant that Retford had successfully reinvented itself as a communications hub in little more than a generation. The White Hart was one of the big winners, all too happy to take in extra coaching traffic. In recent years it has lain empty. The good news is that it has recently been restored and reopened. The bad? It's been given a head-scratchingly different name – The Herbalist. Still, head through the carriage arch on Bridgegate and you'll find traditional paraphernalia like a coachman's mounting block and a yard bell. Outside, I like the painted sign on the corner brickwork – even if I don't like the numbers. Bold black letters tell us that London is 144½ miles in one direction; York 55 miles in the other. Still less than 150 miles from London? It feels as if it should be more. This afternoon, cycling is in danger of turning into a slog.

I cross the well-named River Idle and head across open country toward The Bell at Barnby Moor. Barnby Moor was where the diverted route rejoined the older Great North Road. It simply had to because The Bell is in anyone's top ten of Great North Road inns.

The Bell – technically Ye Old Bell Hotel & Restaurant – looks magnificent today and was once even more so. Inside it's so incredibly timeless that it feels less like a hotel and more like a giant country house where guests just happen to stay. Its rooms are dominated by candelabra, racing prints and monumental fireplaces. Gents, make sure you visit the loos. A recent renovation uncovered the original stable yard cobbles, now kept lit beneath toughened glass because, according to the plaque, it was so "evocative of the days of thundering horses, stagecoaches, notorious highwaymen and hospitality of bygone years." These guys speak my language.

The Bell was also one of the best examples in the country of a coaching inn sustained by an entire village ecosystem. Coaches needed horses, which in turn needed stabling. The young foals could be found in the paddocks nearby, while a large farm was needed to grow enough hay and corn to keep them all fed. Traffic on the Great North Road meant there were once 120 horses at The Bell with stabling for 80 more at a subsidiary inn down the road. Perhaps particularly in this sort of place the arrival of the coaches was an eagerly anticipated event. Believe it or not, there was coach-spotting before there was train-spotting – with the driver the star of the show. Innkeepers and passengers alike were in awe of these "coachies". Harper refers to the observations of the nineteenth-century American writer Washington Irving, who produced a vivid portrait of one of the breed:

"He enjoys great consequence and consideration along the road. The moment he arrives where horses are to be changed, he throws down the reins with something of an air and abandons the cattle to the care of an ostler; his duty being merely to drive them from one stage to another. He rolls about the inn-yard with an air of absolute lordliness. He is generally surrounded by an admiring throng. These all look up to him as to an oracle; treasure up his cant phrases; echo his opinions about horses and other topics of jockey lore; and above all endeavour to imitate his air and carriage. Every ragamuffin that has a coat to his back thrusts his hands in the pockets, rolls in his gait, talks slang and is an embryo coachy."

It wasn't just ragamuffins who were impressed. Young bucks from the gentry longed to try their hand at "the ribbons" as the reins were known. And many a coachy could be persuaded to offer unofficial tuition if the price was right. In this part of the world one of those young bucks was a man called Henry Beever. Now fast forward a few years to the mid-nineteenth century. The Bell, in its remote location, has been left high and dry by the rise of the railways. But Beever has come into some money. He buys the pub and converts it into his own home. But he never forgot the building's original purpose and, crucially, saved it from being subdivided. In this state The Bell survived the 60-odd years between the decline of the stage coach and the rise of the motor car. By 1905 it had been reopened as "a hotel for touring motorists", which is more or less what it remains to this day.

I push on. My body seems to accept that it exists only to turn pedals. A nagging pain over the left knee comes and goes, but it's manageable. Overall my muscles and I seem to have come to some sort of deal. They won't down tools. I won't push my luck. Without really admitting it, I am now working almost exclusively off the middle chain ring. It's probably costing me a couple of miles an hour, but it's keeping the show on the road. Torworth is followed by Ranskill and then I coast down from Scrooby Top to Scrooby village. These are the last knockings of Nottinghamshire. Boisterous, bolshie Yorkshire lies ahead and I wonder how local pride here compares to the noisy neighbour next door.

In my mind's eye the Welcome to Yorkshire road sign is a must-have Facebook photo, but sadly I am welcomed to Doncaster instead. I'm not in Doncaster, I am in Bawtry – the traditional southern gateway to Yorkshire – but it also forms the border of the South Yorkshire Metropolitan Borough of Doncaster. That might be good for local democracy, but it's terrible for ceremonial photos. As if to make up for it, the first house across the border is called No 1 Yorkshire. That's more like it.

I expected Bawtry to be a bit anonymous. Perhaps I had been paying too much attention to Harper, who waxed mournfully on what he saw as the town's inevitable decline. The main coaching inn had been The Crown which was of course on the Great North Road itself:

The Crown is still a prominent feature of Bawtry's now empty street, a street whose width is a revelation of the space once considered necessary and now altogether superfluous; just as the long pillared range of stableyards beyond the old coach archway of the inn itself has now become.

The town, he concluded, "is a monument to the Has Been".

Well, no longer. I arrive in the early evening to find The Crown doing a roaring trade with happy, shiny people spilling out from every entrance. Drivers jockey for the few remaining parking places on Harper's superfluous space. A palpable Friday night prosperity hangs in the air.

"Bawtry is basically the posh bit of Doncaster," explains the parking attendant from his booth.

"See all these Range Rovers and Mercs, they're all here for the decent restaurants. You can pay a fortune here if you want."

It's true. From rural North Nottinghamshire, I've crossed into another world. But I am also even deeper into the Northern conversational bubble. I hadn't approached the parking attendant, I'd simply been taking photos of The Crown. But that was enough.

"Excuse me fella, but what the chuffing hell are you doing taking photos of that. Has thou not seen a pub before."

I might have made up the "thou". I definitely haven't made up the "chuffing". I explain my mission and am given grudging respect for my ambition, if not my sanity. Five minutes later I know where everything is and what everyone does. The Visit Yorkshire tourist board need to sign him up.

I stop taking chuffing photos and find my way around the corner to the village of Austerfield and my bed for the night. It turns out that Home Farm B&B is very much a home from home. I don't just get a room, I get a suite for my money. There's crisp, white linen on the bed at one end, a TV, sofa and kitchen at the other.

Brother-in-law Dave has been out of contact all day. But he eventually turns up on the Harley with my kit. Far from enjoying the byways of the old Great North Road, he's got delayed at home and has simply hurtled up the modern A1 in a hurry. I tell him a modified version of my Downtown wobble and get the full lecture on where I'm going wrong food-wise. It's particularly galling because he's absolutely right. By 7 p.m. he's heading home and by 9.30 p.m. I'm tucked up.

Whatever happens next, at least I can say I made it to Yorkshire.

DAY FIVE

AUSTERFIELD TO WETHERBY

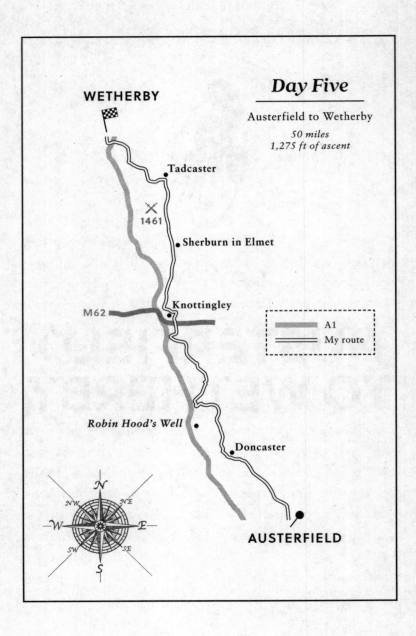

WETHERBY

Day Five

Austerfield to Wetherby

50 miles
1,275 ft of ascent

● Tadcaster

✕
1461

● Sherburn in Elmet

Knottingley

M62 ●

A1
My route

Robin Hood's Well ●

● Doncaster

N
NW NE
W E
SW SE
S

AUSTERFIELD

Dawn breaks early. I only know because this new outdoor version of me seems to work to a different body clock. I get out of bed gingerly, scared that some part of my body will have seized up, but all four limbs appear to be in reasonable working order. Looking around in the half light of half past five, Home Farm feels palatial. For the same sort of money as a pokey hotel room further south, you really do get... space. My hosts leave everything you could possibly need for breakfast in a fridge within the kitchenette. After yesterday's little incident I make sure nothing gets wasted. Over tea and toast, I spread the map out across the coffee table to appreciate that all of Yorkshire lies ahead of me. Famously, the old county has more acres than there are letters in the Bible.

I then turn my attention to Austerfield's most famous son – the Pilgrim Father William Bradford, whose religious zeal had burned from a young age. He was confident enough to have joined a secret congregation down the road at

Scrooby by the age of 12 – despite having lost his mother, his father and grandfather. These so-called Separatists didn't want to reform the Church of England from within, they were committed to setting up their own alternative. But this was a time when the concept of freedom of religion simply didn't exist. Bradford's spiritual conviction would ultimately lead to him abandoning the country altogether, setting sail in 1620 for America on board the famous *Mayflower*. Once across the Atlantic, he went on to write *Of Plymouth Plantation* – the definitive history of the settlement he helped found. Perhaps inevitably, his name is better known there than here, but Austerfield does its bit. A stained-glass window in Bradford's honour was unveiled in 1992 at the village church – albeit the church he chose to reject. In fairness, he was baptised here and a plaque talks of the sickly child turning to the Bible and becoming a devout Christian. Further down the same road the Butten Meadow housing development takes a twenty-first century viewpoint – honouring the victim rather than a leader. Servant William Butten was the only person to have died during the *Mayflower*'s voyage; he is said to have perished within sight of land. Well-crafted Delft tiles show both the ship and the coast of New England. Nevertheless don't run away with the idea that the Pilgrim Fathers pull in the punters in this part of Yorkshire. Certainly at Home Farm, they say they don't massively benefit from American tourism. Their guests are mostly Brits and Europeans.

I'm on the road by 9 a.m. Once again I've got virtually nothing in the pannier because my sister and her partner have taken over the *directeur sportif* role from Dave. They've collected my stuff and will meet me at Darrington for lunch. On the grounds that I should never be cycling south, I avoid the direct route back to Bawtry, skirting Robin Hood Airport before rejoining the GNR to the north of the town. In the old days they reckoned that this stretch was the finest in all England. Author Tom Bradley extolled its virtues in *The Old Coaching Days in Yorkshire*, published – with slightly rose-tinted spectacles – in 1889:

"Many are the times that opposition coaches have raced over this beautiful bit of road. No fear of any collision here, for the roadway is wide enough for six coaches to drive abreast, and no better opportunity can offer for a team to make up for lost ground or gain an advantage over its opponent."

Today what Bradley called the "macadamised surface" has shrunk while the grass verges have grown. These days a separate bike lane wouldn't go amiss. Then suburbia pounces. I start to think that I have negotiated so many Great North Road towns that I might just have got my eye in. Can I really start to predict what will come next? A park and ride by way of welcome, of course. Perhaps an old golf course, complete with mini-mansions. A big bypass to cross – in this case the M18. Schools from the 1960s normally appear at the same time as bus lanes, accompanied by the odd petrol station and a speed camera before you reach the Victorian terraces. Doncaster largely fits the bill, before throwing a spanner in the works by having an enormous racecourse exactly where I imagined the town centre would be.

"Donny" is rightly proud of its history in this regard. Horses have been raced on the Town Moor for perhaps 500 years and its most famous trophy dates back to 1776. In fact the St Leger is one of the five most prestigious races of the flat racing season and the only one to be held in the north of England. (The other four classics are shared by Epsom in Surrey and Newmarket in Suffolk.) So in any normal September the course is happily heaving throughout a four-day festival. In contrast, it's utterly deserted as I cycle past in mysteriously light early-morning traffic; mysterious until I remember that it's a Saturday. Unlike a football or a cricket ground, there are no fences or gates to stop me trespassing. So for that reason alone I find myself crossing the turf and leaning the bike up against the running rails for a gratuitous selfie. Then it's back onto the route the coaches would have taken along tree-lined Bennetthorpe and Georgian South Parade. All told, it's an elegant approach.

Now a zealous convert to the importance of calorific top-ups, I have a second breakfast in the town centre. But just ordering some porridge turns into a life-affirming five-minute chat. Like the parking attendant at Bawtry, the café staff are fantastically welcoming. All this bonhomie encourages me to stay a little longer so I search out Doncaster Museum – which also revels in the racing. Every year a new trophy was put up for the Gold Cup and as a result the cabinets heave with eighteenth- and nineteenth-century equestrian bling.

Beyond the monolithic Frenchgate shopping centre I catch sight of a long bridge over what I assume to be the River Don. In fact, North Bridge crosses a mass of railway lines and it's difficult to spot the Don Navigation squeezed in alongside. Doncaster survived the decline of the coaching age by the simple expedient of becoming a railway town. Its future was assured when the Great Northern Railway moved its works here in 1853. At its height, more than 4,000 people worked at what everyone called "The Plant", collectively building more than 2,500 locomotives including the legendary *Flying Scotsman* and *Mallard*. The museum is good on all this too. I'd never realised that it was the surrounding coal mines that meant the town became the centre of such a spidery web of branch lines. King Coal brought prosperity until a wave of closures toward the end of the last century.

"Today the town is experiencing a revival as it emerges from the trauma caused by the closure of so many coal mines," runs the museum's commentary.

Note the use of "emerges" rather than "emerged" and "trauma" instead of "changes". Strong words from a town with a proud history.

————

I cross North Bridge and then another spanning the Don proper to find myself at the mother of all roundabouts; one so sprawling that another of Doncaster's ubiquitous railways runs right through the middle. This point once marked the parting of the ways for northbound traffic. The right-hand fork held the Great North Road title in the early days when most coaches made it no further than York. But once the technology had improved enough to make Edinburgh a realistic destination, a new route emerged. These coaches would shave perhaps 20 miles off the total distance by heading to first Ferrybridge and then Wetherby.

"As both can equally claim to be an integral part of the Great North Road, it is necessary to go back these sixty-three miles to that town and explore the route," the ever-thorough Harper tells his readers.

Clearly York has its attractions, but I'd already decided to push on to Wetherby. The fact that Harper didn't like the next section of the York route was one factor. He described the run into Selby as being across:

... a flat, watery, treeless, featureless plain, its negative qualities tempered by the frankly mean and ugly villages

on the way, and criss-crossed by railways, sluggish rivers and unlovely canals. So utterly without interest is the road, that a crude girder-bridge or a gaunt and forbidding flour-mill remain vividly impressed upon the mental retina for the lack of any other outstanding objects.

In the end a dual carriageway in the wrong place forces me into a hybrid of the two routes, passing the suburb of Bentley in the process. Bentley is the first former pit village that I've knowingly passed through, so a detour to the colliery itself seems appropriate. But that's not as easy as you might think. Ordnance Survey might lovingly chronicle every ancient monument and battle site, but it doesn't mark former mines. I end up asking for directions from a man on his way back from the paper shop.

"Excuse me, do you know where the colliery used to be?"

"Pit, you mean?"

"Sorry, yes the pit."

I've never felt so Southern in all my life. But as ever in this part of the world, people are happy to talk. When I ask if any of his relatives had worked at the mine, I'm told that one had died down there. The Bentley Colliery Disaster of 1978 saw seven people killed as the result of an underground train crash. These so-called Paddy Trains would ferry miners in one direction and coal in the other. That accident happened almost 47 years to the day after an even more deadly tragedy in 1931 when 45 people lost their lives after a gas explosion. Such were the horrors and the dangers of a working life underground.

The pit itself closed in 1994 with the buildings being demolished soon afterwards. As a result all I can see is a "community woodland" where people go to walk their dogs. I feel a strange contrast between a landscape shorn of its mining history while memories continue to burn brightly among residents. By comparison, in the nearby village of Askern, they've recently moved the giant pit wheel to a prominent site on the edge of an old boating lake – an obvious symbol of the mining heritage.

Incidentally, Askern is where Harper, as a Southerner, really starts to let rip:

> Askerne, (sic) in a situation of great natural beauty amidst limestone rocks and lakes, and with the advantage of possessing medicinal springs, has been, like most Yorkshire villages, made hideous by its houses and cottages, inconceivably ugly to those who have not seen what abominable places Yorkshire folk are capable of building and living in.

Steady on, sir…

From Bentley I pass Toll Bar and then turn left at what I think is Owston but isn't, and get thoroughly lost on the back roads. Those unnaturally shaped hills, I now realise, are grassed-over pit heaps. In Carcroft, I ask a man in his thirties for directions to the village of Campsall.

"Campsall?" he spits out.

"What, by bike? From here?"

I've had this before at various places across the country. Some people live such incredibly local lives that they can't conceive of a four-mile journey by bike.

"Yeh, I've to get to Campsall and then up to Ferrybridge. I'm trying to avoid the main roads."

"Campsall? God, I haven't been there for years."

He isn't winding me up, the village is simply beyond his ken – and that's playing havoc with his navigation skills. For devilment, I tell him I'm cycling on to Edinburgh. That doesn't faze him at all. But Campsall...

In the end I meander west through Old Skellow and Burghwallis before finding Campsall and pushing north. This area was once part of the ancient Forest of Barnsdale – reputedly the haunt of Robin Hood. Somewhere around here the outlaw humiliated the Bishop of Hereford, relieving him of a large sum of money and making him dance for his supper. I find little evidence of a forest, but between the two alternative routes north, I certainly escape the traffic – even if it's at the expense of several unnecessary miles.

Over on the modern A1 there's another reminder at a hamlet called Robin Hood's Well. Thirsty travellers have stopped here for centuries, drawn by the quality of the spring water. An ornate well house built to cover the spring is all that survives. Sadly it's been moved from its original spot – a victim of one of the A1's many upgrades.

But while the modern pilgrim's desire for drink remains unquenched, the helpful information board includes a poem singing its praises from almost 400 years ago:

> *Thirst knows neither name nor measure*
> *Robin Hood's Well was my treasure*
> *In a common dish enchained*
> *My furious thirst restrained*
> *And because I drunk the deeper*
> *I paid two farthings to the keeper.*

Those memories certainly tie in with a seventeenth-century writer, the diarist John Evelyn, who described people sitting in a stone chair and drinking the water with the help of an iron ladle. It's enough to send a shiver down public health officials' spines – whatever the era.

Harper, ever the contrarian, wasn't impressed. He described the well house as being "very ugly". In fact he was more taken with the graffiti, paying tribute to the number of wayfarers "who, in two centuries have carved every available inch of its surface with their names".

Once this was a busy spot with coaching inns on either side of the road; now, truth be told, it's a bit soulless. But it does provide another piece of circumstantial evidence that, whatever they like to tell you in Nottinghamshire, this was

Robin Hood's old manor. And, health concerns aside, I like the thought of an ancient spring on an ancient road. It adds to that sense of pilgrimage – encouraging us to remember those who have journeyed this way before...

―――――

I've left my sister Caroline and her partner Colin to organise the lunchtime venue. And while I normally go for town centres, they've gone for a golf club in the middle of nowhere. They haven't paid enough attention to the contours either. To my complaining legs, our rendezvous point is perched needlessly high on a hill. Then again, hills are becoming harder to avoid. Established in the early 1990s, the Mid Yorkshire Golf Club on the outskirts of Darrington still feels rather new – as though the fairways and greens have yet to be fully accepted by the landscape. I lock the bike outside (no doubt unnecessarily) and realise that it feels strange to walk into the home of the sweater and slacks brigade when I'm sporting pure MAMIL. Never has my Lycra felt so shiny. Caroline and Colin are well-ensconced in the restaurant. Colin has nearly finished his pint, but one of the many good things about being a cyclist is that no one feels they can complain when you are late. Over lunch we plot my next move.

―――――

If the A1 is the most glamorous modern road in the country, I'll allow the M62 to take second place. What the trans-Pennine motorway lacks in history it makes up for in sheer connectability. Over 107 rolling miles, it links the Lancashire rivals of Liverpool and Manchester to Leeds and Bradford. But it also connects so many other decent towns and cities that the distance signposts read like football league tables – Huddersfield, Oldham and Rochdale. The road's strategic purpose was to go coast to coast, but it actually pulls up short at each end, politely downgrading itself to a dual carriageway. You could blame hesitant planners, but I see it as a mark of the road's charm.

From Darrington this west-east motorway looks a formidable barrier to a south-north traveller – at least on a small-scale map. Thankfully, a pinch and a zoom on Colin's smartphone reveal chinks in its defences. Within a mile of the golf club there's a track which appears to have its own narrow bridge under the motorway. Fully fuelled by a golf club Full English breakfast, I decide it's worth a go. The track's called Leys Lane and some minor off-roading gets me within shouting distance of a now-screaming M62. I'm now in the kind of no-man's land that you often find at the periphery of Big Roads. The traffic is loud. Everything else is spookily quiet. My track ducks under the motorway next to a vast quarry where the surface is too rough for cycling. Yes, I've invested in Schwalbe Marathon Plus tyres, but no, somehow I don't fancy even the tiny risk of getting a puncture. Instead I dismount, my cleats crunching in the chalky soil.

I'm now in Knottingley: England Lane, Knottingley. And one of the most desolate of urban landscapes I've found in all of England so far. Once there was simply a bridge across the River Aire at neighbouring Ferrybridge. Later they dug out the Aire and Calder Navigation to transport coal to the River Ouse at Goole while great chunks of limestone were shipped in the other direction. Railways followed, with accidents of timing and geography making this a convenient point for sweeping junctions – and more of those empty zones in between. The A1 was first dualled and then moved bodily westwards. Then there's the M62, its junction with the new A1 now a geometric whirl. Believe it or not, a Neolithic henge is partially buried somewhere beneath its flyovers. Just to the east, Kellingley Colliery was opened in 1965. "Big K" was the last deep coal mine to operate in the country. On England Lane I cross a branch line next to a glassworks – another Knottingley speciality. There are also chemical factories and power stations. You get the picture. Several generations of industrial revolution have imposed their will and the end result is not always pretty.

I confess that for the only time during my entire trip I feel conspicuous cycling on a touring bike through the housing estates – an obvious outsider. A lone teenager, eyes sunk deep into his hoodie, sits low on a kerb and watches me all the way. It's early afternoon and for some reason this part of town is otherwise deserted. But redemption isn't far away as I turn a corner and hear noises that I recognise but can't quite place. It's cricket. Of course it's cricket, it's leather on willow. Tucked away at the Banks Garth Cricket Ground, Knottingley Town Second XI is in the process of beating a neighbouring village – with great shouts and back-slapping in the process.

The most famous landmarks in this area are the cooling towers which made up Ferrybridge C Power Station. I always loved passing them on the A1's original route, fascinated by their other-worldliness. The station stopped production in 2016, with the demolition of the towers following in 2019. Crowds gathered in the rain as the titans first shrank in size, before warping in shape and finally imploding in a puff of smoke. It was a powerful symbol of the British energy industry getting out of coal and moving to something greener. Now just three towers remain – and their future is uncertain.

I cross a canal and find my way down to the towpath, belatedly realising that I'm on an island between the navigation and the original River Aire. After the noise and the pollution of the M62 this is more peaceful – thick scrub on one side, the water on the other. The land narrows to an isthmus from which I escape by way of a tiny bridge next to the lock-keeper's house, singularly unsuitable for bikes. Back on the mainland a street confusingly called The Square has a pleasingly old-fashioned air to it – as long as you ignore the flyover. This had been a convenient point to cross the River Aire since 1198 – and was presumably the mooring point for a ferry before that. The bridge we see today was completed in 1804 as a reaction to the ever-increasing number of coaches. Now open to just cyclists and pedestrians, it seems extraordinary that its arches carried the full weight of Great North Road traffic until the early 1960s. Close by, a curiously shaped building stands on its own. It's that rare thing, a surviving toll house. The unusual design is to allow windows on just about every side – visibility was all-important for a keen-eyed taker of tolls.

Give me a drone camera and I could summarise an awful lot of Great North Road history from here. The river as a major obstacle. The stone bridge and the toll house as the first-generation solution with goods carried by barge. Hover a little higher to include the concrete bridge carrying the A162 and the modern services to the south, with the M62 now taking west-east traffic. That's the opening titles for *Great North Road – The Movie* all sorted out then.

I cross the bridge, trying and failing to find any last evidence of The Swan on the northern bank. The inn was described by Harper as being the most luxurious in the north of England. The gentry stayed here in great numbers; among them the protagonist in surely the most tragic of all Great North Road stories. Charles Frederick Vanburgh was travelling south from the inn in 1781 after a trip to Scotland. When staff realised that he had left his purse behind, a member of staff called Gervase Thompson was dispatched on horseback to catch him up. Within a mile of Ferrybridge, he approached him at the carriage window, calling out "Your purse, your purse, sir".

But it was 7 p.m. on a dark February evening. And, in the words of the *Leeds Intelligenser*, Vanburgh "from the noise of the carriage, imagining he demanded his purse, let down the window and instantly shot him dead". He didn't realise the truth of the matter until he had reached Doncaster. Vanburgh offered Mr Thompson's widow five guineas immediately and later agreed to pay her ten pounds a year for the rest of her life. Later a coroner's jury returned a verdict of self-defence. The full story is recounted on a website dedicated to the history of Georgian Britain. "I can't help but wonder," says the first comment after the article, "what the coroner's jury would have found had the barman accidentally shot the lord, instead of the other way round."

From the bridge I can see that the Great North Road is once again a dual carriageway, so I'm dragged east onto the Tadcaster road. A cast-iron milepost near the village of Brotherton immediately reassures me that it does have some sort of pedigree – the Tadcaster and Doncaster turnpike from the 1740s as it turns out. But soon Caroline and Colin flag me down; Colin's got the map out. This isn't the Great North Road, he says, shouldn't you be heading west? The tenets of the Lemsford Doctrine – which had last troubled me in St Neots – chime in my mind, but my legs are weary. I decide to plod on regardless – but slightly guiltily. A little later I dig out Harper. On page 68 of his second volume he gives the Ferrybridge to Tadcaster route his blessing as an authorised Great North Road alternative. Thank you C. G. H., I owe you one.

My turnpike never seems to be flat, but the mileposts are punctilious. Picked out in black capitals on whitewashed stone, Tadcaster is first 11¼ miles away, then 10¼, then 9¼. They're fixed firmly but always visibly into lush green verges alongside arable fields. Despite the odd gradient, it's hardly a typical Yorkshire landscape – more big skies than anything dale-like or moor-ish.

There's plenty of traffic; it's one of those single-track A-roads where drivers are tempted up to 50 or 60 mph. And if I've got my eye in for Great North Road suburbia, I've now got my ear in on engine noise too. The sound of a throaty 4 x 4 is what I dread most, particularly those towing long, empty trailers. In my experience these guys never give you much space. There's an initial whoosh as the driver changes gear to accelerate past, then a nerve-shredding finale as the trailer rattles on through. Respite comes in the shape of South Milford and Sherburn in Elmet where a new bypass funnels off the through traffic. But whatever the traffic I am now rather robotically going through the motions: left knee, right knee, left knee, right knee – weary pistons running out of steam.

North of Sherburn I rejoin and then divert from the main drag to see the site of the biggest battle you've never heard of. The Battle of Towton is a Wars of the Roses epic. Some say that 30,000 people died there in 1461. And although such high numbers are dismissed by some modern historians, all agree it was peculiarly bloody. The battle certainly saw the Yorkists defeat the Lancastrians, confirming the young Edward IV's place on the throne.

The road to the battlefield is open, hilly and heading in the wrong direction. But Caroline and Colin are waiting for me, so it's got to be done. And of course it is worth it. The main fighting took place to the east of the road we're now on. But the official viewpoint is to the west, near an ancient memorial cross. While thousands of Lancastrians died on the main battlefield, many more were cut down as they tried to flee across the land close to the River Cock. These killing fields are clearly visible from our vantage point. In effect the Lancastrians were trying to climb their way out of a steep-sided bowl. The fact that the area is still called Bloody Meadow tells you what happened next.

We return to the village of Towton for re-fuelling at the Rockingham Arms. And it really is fuel. I don't take much delight in the coffee and cakes and I'm not particularly good company either. Caroline kindly wants me to rest awhile. But Wetherby remains a stubborn 12 miles away and I want to get on with it. There's no point denying that cycling can sometimes feel a bit soul-destroying. My mind isn't particularly willing, my flesh is certainly weak – but an Airbnb booking says I have to plough on. Thankfully it's relatively plain sailing toward Tadcaster. And if I wasn't already convinced that I was in the north, the road signs are keen to confirm it. Solid northern consonants are required for Ulleskelf, Grimston and Scarthingwell. None of them would want to be seen dead with a Surrey post code.

Tadcaster itself is dominated by three breweries. The industry flourished here because of its hard water, taken from limestone springs known as popple-wells – possibly and onomatopoeically because they "popped" or bubbled. In coaching times, if coach passengers weren't drinking Tadcaster Bitter, they were being offered popple-water at their tables. Today, visitors arriving from the south are welcomed by a magnificent Willy Wonka-style factory – the home of the John Smith's brewery. It's classic late Victorian; tall multi-storeyed buildings of rusticated sandstone. But this traditional building is now owned by Heineken, which brews Kronenburg 1664 and Newcastle Brown Ale here as well as the eponymous bitter.

Further down the high street I find the Old Brewery owned by Samuel Smith's. Two branches of the Smith family went their separate ways in the late nineteenth century and while Team John has gone corporate Team Samuel is determinedly old school. It remains a big landowner in the town and it's still run by a member of the same family – Humphrey Smith is the latest custodian. Here, they haven't changed their strain of yeast since the 1800s. The Old Brewery Bitter is still transported in oak casks made by full-time coopers and many of those casks are delivered to local pubs by carts pulled by shire horses. I keep going down the high street as far as a bridge across the River Wharfe. Famously, this was partially washed away during the floods of December 2015. It took a year to rebuild. Connecting the banks by a temporary footbridge was seen as a top priority, yet when Humphrey Smith was asked for permission to use his land he refused, saying the bridge was "wasteful proposed public expenditure".

I leave feeling rather confused by Tadcaster. It has bijou shops here, beautiful but boarded-up properties there. It feels like a town waiting for a kick up the backside.

I strike out for Wetherby along a road which roughly follows the Wharfe to Boston Spa. Blue and yellow bicycles hang at crazy angles from shops and lamp posts, reminding me that this has been the route for a Tour de Yorkshire race. I cross the Wharfe at Boston and head into Wetherby on an old railway path next to the racecourse. Somehow, Wetherby comes under the purview of Leeds City Council, but it couldn't be less metropolitan. It's an old-fashioned market town – once rugged, now gentrified – built on a solid limestone ridge overlooking the Wharfe. Most of the buildings are constructed from the same stone – a creamy, oolitic magnesian limestone, paler than the kind I saw back in Stamford.

Historically it was of course a Great North Road town, but it was also something more ancient and elemental – a drovers' town. For hundreds of years many roads across Britain sporadically teemed with people driving animals to market. And not just the local market. Drovers thought nothing of taking cattle and sheep from Scotland all the way down to Smithfield in London, averaging at least 12 miles a day.

Given the value of their mobile cargo, drovers were trusted men; a breed apart with their own rules and customs. Where they could, they kept away from other traffic – often by sticking to broad tracks across high ground. In this way thousands of animals were driven from the hillier and wetter terrain of Scotland and Wales to the population centres in the south and the east. But at some point they needed to hit a main road and head due south. Unusually, the Great North Road was wide enough to be drover-friendly. And many Scottish contingents joined it here. According to the late nineteenth-century author Tom Bradley, the numbers were extraordinary:

"At certain seasons of the year the numbers of cattle that came south along the Great North Road were something prodigious. Many a time from sunrise to sunset have the streets of Wetherby never for one minute been free from cattle, as drove after drove passed through the town, and some idea of the magnitude of those droves may be gathered from the fact that individual herds have been known to pack the road for fully a mile of its length."

For Wetherby – and other GNR towns in the vicinity – where there was muck, there was brass. The drovers needed to shoe their cattle for life on the highway. Local farriers were only too keen to help – at a price. Today the old Drovers' Inn, just south of the bridge in Wetherby, is a listed building split into a number of cottages. Presumably the land running down to the river behind was where both herd and flock were corralled. I try to imagine a sea of sheep, a cacophony of baas, being funnelled into the right places.

"This is a hard-featured, stony town; still as of old chiefly concerned with cattle-raising and cattle-dealing," wrote Harper.

"[It's] crowded on market days with farmers and drovers driving bargains or swearing at the terrified efforts of beasts and sheep to find their way into the shops and inns."

But as we walk up to the town centre this Saturday evening, it presents a very different picture with plenty of people cheerfully spilling out of the pubs and restaurants.

Once again Caroline has the job of sorting out the meal and she's picked an Italian – the smart Sant' Angelo. It takes me a while to realise that this is actually The Angel of old – Wetherby's premier coaching inn. We get to enjoy the smart bow windows which have protruded onto the high street for centuries, while drinkers are relegated to the first floor. In the old days this place was a blessed relief for northern-bound coach passengers; they had around an hour to take some exercise and eat a hearty meal. Those taking the *Highflyer* service to Edinburgh even got a new coach.

These days it is entirely fitting that The Angel has become Sant' Angelo, given the pub's Second World War history. There were German and Italian prisoner of war camps in the countryside nearby. The Angel was the only pub in the town which agreed to serve them. The landlord argued they were simply fellow human beings caught up in a war not of their own making. Seventy-plus years later the pasta is excellent as are the ice creams. Afterwards we walk down to the bridge in time to see the last vestiges of a sunset beyond the weir. As we head back via the town hall, I spot a stage coach motif around the notice board. Alongside, a crucial fact: London is 200 miles south while Edinburgh is 200 miles north. After five days on the road I'm halfway there.

DAY SIX

WETHERBY TO NORTHALLERTON

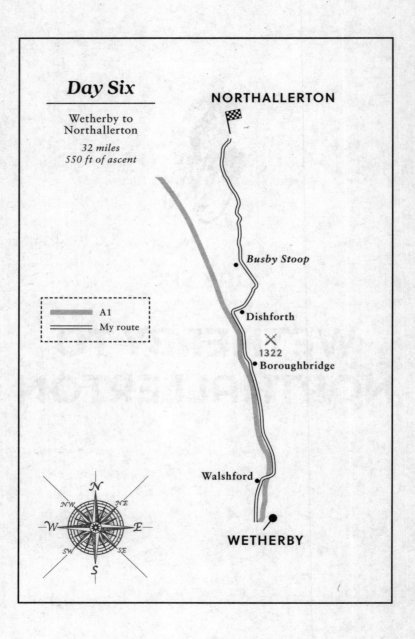

Day Six

Wetherby to
Northallerton

32 miles
550 ft of ascent

NORTHALLERTON

Busby Stoop

Dishforth

✕
1322
Boroughbridge

━━━ A1
═══ My route

Walshford

WETHERBY

N
NW NE
W E
SW SE
S

I sleep fitfully at a thoroughly underwhelming Airbnb on the outskirts of Wetherby. The bed linen clearly hasn't been washed, there are no proper curtains at the window and missing slats cause my mattress to sag. In fact the whole experience had been off-putting from the start. Via the app, the householder had warned me that he wouldn't be there, but a key would be left out. So, the previous night, I had let myself in to this perfect stranger's house, leaned the bike against the banisters and tiptoed upstairs to the spare bedroom. In the dead of night I awake from a dream in which a burglar had tried to get in, rattling the front door as he did so. When I finally give up on sleep at about 7 a.m., I discover that the dream had been real. My host has unexpectedly returned in the early hours but is unable to let himself in because of a dodgy door latch. He has since come back for a second time and is waiting patiently outside. I let him back into his own house and we exchange awkward pleasantries in the kitchen. He's very polite about being locked out, but I'm too cowardly to tell him what I think of his facilities. In summary, I can't get out quickly enough.

Wetherby, understandably on a Sunday, has yet to wake up. Only Costa Coffee is open for business, but I'm far from being the first customer. The place is swarming with cyclists out for the obligatory Sunday run. Bloody part-timers. For the first time since Look Mum No Hands, I actually fit in because *everyone* is noisily clip-clopping around in cleated shoes while wolfing down cake and coffee. Most are doing west-east journeys so their miles will be hillier and harder-won than mine. Other than that, I don't get beyond a few gruff acknowledgements. Within the cycling fraternity of Yorkshire a solemn "How do?" goes a long way at this hour.

Back on the road, I cycle back past Sant' Angelo and head up the Deighton Road. While The Angel used to claim it was halfway between London and Edinburgh, the actual spot is a mile or so to the north at Kirk Deighton. Here, outside a pub called The Old Fox, Harper tells us that the "milestone told the same tale on either face". This was a big deal for the drovers who would celebrate with a ritual drink – even though they were unlikely to have come all the way from Edinburgh. Both the pub and the milestone are long gone, though I like to think the latter lies in someone's garden. In my utopian future where the Great North Road becomes a cycling superhighway, The Old Fox would rise again as The Halfway House – a bike hostel for long-distance cyclists. They could even include beds with a full complement of slats.

I spend ten minutes scrabbling around in the undergrowth, hunting for the remains of the old building – it's becoming rather a habit on this journey. I convince myself I'm in the right place, but maybe it's just wishful thinking. In the planning of the trip, I'd promised myself a drink here in honour of the drovers. But it's 8.30 a.m. on a Sunday morning so that pledge is quietly jettisoned as I continue along the Great North Road in its new guise as the A168. To my surprise, there's a semi-official bike path running alongside. Judging by the paint markings poking out from beneath the weeds, I really am on the original road. And as a bonus, there's a thick hedge of tumbling May blossom between me and the traffic.

It's so secluded that I stop for no other reason than to enjoy the solitude – easy like Sunday morning. Rather guiltily, I run my eye around the geometry of the bike. Before I set off, I'd resolved to clean it daily. Well, that just hasn't happened. I've yet to have a puncture, the pressure on both tyres feel fine to my touch and the unfashionably long mudguards really are protecting every other surface. This bike is proving to be admirably low maintenance. I also pay attention for the first time to some steel knitting needles attached to the chainstay. I faintly recall the patter from the salesman. "If you're stuck in Darkest Peru, and you buckle your wheel, there will be always be someone who can fix it as long as you've got spare spokes." Ah, yes, spokes.

This path keeps me out of trouble as far as Walshford, where the Great North Road crosses another Yorkshire Dales river, the Nidd, following hard on the heels of the Wharfe at Wetherby. From now until the Scottish border, you feel the presence of the Pennines even if you don't often see them, as river after river takes its turn to cross the GNR on its way to the North Sea. I'm old enough to have had the *I-Spy* books as a kid. How about a Great North Road version complete with a list of rivers, as well as coaching inns and battle sites?

The hamlet of Walshford has been bypassed not once but twice over the years so that three northbound roads now lie almost side by side. The oldest has a parkland estate to one side and a collection of buildings belonging to The Bridge Inn on the other. In the old days it traded on its proximity to the main road; to a certain extent that still holds true, but now a bit of quiet doesn't go amiss as it enjoys its latest incarnation as a "hotel and spa".

Here, you don't need much of an imagination to feel the centuries fall away and see the mail coaches clatter through. The old road likes to throw in a cameo appearance like this from time to time – always in unfashionable spots and only if you know what you are looking for. Leaning against the bike, I'm caught daydreaming on this theme by a hotel worker coming out for a cigarette, his very presence embarrassing me back into activity.

After Walshford my road switches to the east of the A1, becoming straight and without sanctuary for the cyclist. The odd car speeds past at 60 mph; a reminder that it's good to get these miles done on a Sunday. Back at Alconbury in Cambridgeshire, I realised that the settlements were getting fewer and further between. This section of road takes that concept to the next level. I feel, if not lonely, then alone for the first time. The road has passed through the M62 population belt and I won't go through another major conurbation until Darlington, some 50 miles to the north. Further on, I stop for a quick breather next to another of the cast-iron mileposts that I'm growing rather fond of. Raising my head from the road, I realise that two of England's national parks are now visible – one on either side. To the west, the spine of the Yorkshire Dales, little more than a watercolour of dark blue on the horizon. To the east the closer, more distinct outline of the North York Moors, a trick of the light making its smoother contours much clearer. In an instant it becomes crystal clear why the Great North Road takes this route. The A1, the A19, the A167 and the East Coast railway line all share the relatively flat Vale of York. Surely as long as Brits have travelled north and south, this has been where we have channelled our major highways.

Then it's Boroughbridge, a market town which has grown in recent years so that there are substantial outskirts to plough through first. Before the town centre I take a short detour to see the three mysterious standing stones known as the Devil's Arrows. No one can really explain their purpose, although some mention a connection with a southernmost summer moonrise. Aligned north-north west to south-south east, the Bronze Age giants are between 18 and 22 feet high, the latter taller than anything at Stonehenge. A fourth stone is said to have been removed in either the late sixteenth or early seventeenth century as Boroughbridge endured a brief phase of Philistinism. In the words of the mapmaker William Camden in his 1607 book *Britannia* it "was lately pulled downe by some that hope, though in vaine, to find treasure". No treasure, but still some grandeur. Although it's a grandeur despite the setting, rather than because of it. You can't help but be disappointed to discover that two of the three stones are behind a fenced-in field of cabbages while the third is marooned on the other side of a minor road. Surely they have to be brought together within a park setting?

All told it's not surprising that local historian Ronald Walker has described the arrows on Boroughbridge Town Council's website as being "among the least understood and most neglected historic monuments in Britain".

Boroughbridge breaks the Great North Road mould by keeping its high street hidden from the main drag. Only the coaching inns were on this thoroughfare, but they were at the centre of an unlikely hub. Making my journey from London to Edinburgh, I'm inclined to forget that there were other coaches heading for other destinations. The *North Briton*, the *Phoenix*, the *Diligence*, the *Expedition* and the

Defence all ran from Leeds to Newcastle via Boroughbridge; the *North Star* went from Leeds to Edinburgh; the *Rapid* from Harrogate to Thirsk and the *Union* from London to Newcastle. Finally, the *Royal Charlotte* from Leeds timed its services to meet both Newcastle and Glasgow coaches in this otherwise inconsequential town. The Crown was at the centre of the web. It's another classic coaching inn which has managed to retain its original footprint. I once stayed here on a cold February evening when snow fell unexpectedly during the night. Cars were banished, twenty-first century sights and sounds disappeared under a cloak of white and were it not for the presenter of Stray FM reading out the school closures, we might have been enjoying our bacon and eggs in Dickensian times. It was wonderful in every way.

But this time I don't even stop for a courtesy coffee, heading instead for the bridge over the River Ure – site of the Battle of Boroughbridge in 1322. Like Empingham back in Rutland, this battle took place directly on the Great North Road. The Earl of Lancaster, rebelling against Edward II, was caught in a pincer movement between the king's soldiers heading up from the south and a force led by Sir Andrew Harclay coming down from the north. Harclay's men blocked both the bridge and a nearby ford. Lancaster tasked the Earl of Hereford with taking the bridge. But, in an incident worthy of *Horrible Histories*, Hereford was killed by a pikeman hidden under the bridge who managed to thrust his spear directly up Hereford's backside. It wasn't a great omen.

THE GREAT NORTH ROAD

Many more men were killed before Lancaster managed to negotiate a truce. And even that proved short-lived. He was later beheaded at Pontefract Castle, with 30 of his followers punished in the same way.

Immediately to the north of the bridge, the Great North Road traffic used to turn right. Nowadays we turn left because the old route lies obliterated under the runway of Dishforth Airfield. The full irony only becomes clear as I cycle along its western perimeter a few miles later. In recent years the airfield itself has become obsolete with weeds poking up through the concrete. So an abandoned Great North Road now lies under an abandoned Second World War airstrip. Perhaps I was paying too much attention to old ghosts here, because the next thing I know I'm on a dual carriageway heading for Thirsk. At Junction 49 it's easily done. For a scary mile and a half I survive on a hard shoulder before re-joining the original Great North Road at Topcliffe, which surprises me by calling its high street "Front Street". To me, Front Streets belong to the north east of England, preferably County Durham. Topcliffe is very much in North Yorkshire, but the road sign suggests I am making good progress. The village is memorable for another reason too; while I exercise the MAMIL's God-given right to do slightly geeky leg stretches against the Methodist church railings, I see my first swifts of the summer screeching overhead.

"Aye, they've been here a few days now," says a passer-by. "Where are you heading?"

"Northallerton – and I'm starving."

"Northallerton? Get yourself down the carvery at The Golden Lion. You canna go wrong."

Summer's here, the swifts have arrived and there's decent food down the road. Excellent.

Somewhere around here, travellers leave the Vale of York for the Vale of Mowbray – and crossing the River Swale at Topcliffe feels as appropriate a boundary as any other. While the Vale of York is seen as an area of intensive arable farming, the Vale of Mowbray has a more intimate scale. One gets the impression that while the tourists head for the high ground of the Dales and the Moors, the locals here are happy to get on with their farming out of the limelight.

To the west of the Swale, the modern A1 temporarily follows the line of Dere Street – the Roman road which ran from York to Scotland through places like Catterick, Bishop Auckland and Corbridge. Running north west rather than north, it is nevertheless dead straight. Meanwhile the original Great North Road stays to the east of the Swale and looks almost entirely unmodernised as I cycle on.

"The remaining 19 miles to Northallerton scarce call for detailed description," wrote Harper.

I have to disagree. The first junction of note is a roundabout with a petrol garage on one side, an Indian restaurant on the other and an unusual name on the map: Busby Stoop. Behind those two words lies a grisly folktale dating back more than 300 years. The restaurant was, until very recently, a pub. In

1702, the pub's landlord was Thomas Busby, a small-time criminal who had married Elizabeth Auty, the daughter of the notorious counterfeiter Daniel Auty of Danotty Hall. Father and son-in-law initially got on well, but later fell out. And one day when Busby returned to his pub the worse for wear, he found Auty sitting in his favourite chair threatening to take Elizabeth back home. There are numerous versions of what happened next, but the most succinct summary I've found comes from journalist Chris Lloyd in a feature for *The Northern Echo* newspaper:

"Thomas ejected Daniel from both chair and pub and later that night crept into the counterfeiter's house and bludgeoned him to death with a hammer. Busby was found guilty of murder and forgery and ordered to be hanged on a gibbet to be erected on the crossroads outside the pub, his body having been first dipped in tar to prolong its decomposition. Before the execution, Thomas was allowed a final drink in his favourite chair. As he left for the hangman's noose, he cursed the chair, saying anyone who sat in it would suffer a premature, painful end."

Curiously, the tale then takes a breather for 200-odd years before a chimney sweep sat in the chair in 1894 and was found hanging from the original post (or stoop) the next day. But the legend really took off during the Second World War when the pub – already renamed The Busby Stoop – became popular with Canadian airmen based at nearby RAF Skipton-on-Swale. Locals said that Royal Canadian

Air Force aircrew who sat in the chair never came back from their bombing missions. From then on, the story kept growing.

Throughout the late 1960s and 1970s there appeared to be a rash of strange tragedies. And when a young builder died after being cajoled into sitting in the chair by his mates, the landlord Tony Earnshaw banished it to the cellar. The final straw came when a delivery man tried it out down there – and died in a road accident soon afterwards. In 1978, Earnshaw donated the accursed chair to a museum – with strict instructions that no one should sit in it.

Busby's chair is now to be found at the community-run Thirsk Museum. Until relatively recently, it was rather hidden away, suspended from the ceiling in the kitchen section – a little out of sight, out of mind. But in 2018 it was moved to pride of place in the front room and hung high on a wall. Crucially no one is allowed to sit on the chair – not even the Japanese film crew who had travelled thousands of miles thinking they could do just that. I visited the museum once and couldn't resist asking the volunteer guide if, really, it wasn't just a load of old nonsense.

"Well, most of those deaths do seem to be coincidental," she said.

Then she fixed me with a rather beadier eye.

"But on the other hand, there do seem to have been rather a lot of them."

I paused, not knowing whether to push the point.

"Put it like this," she continued. "Last winter when it came off those hooks I was happy to polish it, but silly as it sounds, I certainly didn't sit on it."

———

I cycle on through Sandhutton, shadowing the River Wiske northwards. Looking at the OS map, I spot Danotty Hall Farm. It still exists, it seems. So I find myself turning left, crossing the river at tiny Kirby Wiske and heading off down narrow lanes. Eventually I get a look at the farmhouse, but it lies at least half a mile off-road, perched on a hill top. It was this lonely location which helped Auty evade justice as a counterfeiter for so long. I can see why. But the track is too rough and too long for a random bit of cold-calling by a bloke on a bike. Reluctantly, I turn back for the main road.

A few miles later I arrive in Northallerton, which announces itself as the prosperous capital of North Yorkshire with a broad high street and a wide range of shops. It's old-fashioned enough to allow drivers to park directly on the street, but new-fangled enough to have delicatessens and expensive cafés. On a weekday it demands to be described as "bustling". There's a traditional department store, a foodie shop seemingly modelled on Fortnum & Mason and the first bookshop I've seen since Highgate.

As I get closer to the centre, I finally articulate a feeling that's been bubbling up for a while. Stamford, Newark,

Wetherby and now Northallerton; these are all places I've visited before. But now I'm seeing them through different eyes – simply because I am arriving under my own steam. Digging deep into an O-level French vocabulary, I remember the verb "gagner". Gagner – to reach, to earn, to win. I've not just reached Northallerton, I feel as if I've earned the right to be here. This is going to sound ridiculous to anyone who hasn't cycled long-distance, but towns really do feel bigger and better if you've had to crack on through the countryside and the hinterland under your own steam.

The substantial frontage of The Golden Lion dominates the high street. And in case anyone needs reminding of the inn's name, a porch projects onto the pavement complete with fluted Doric columns below and a large statue of a lion above. I like the place from the minute I walk through the door. It's a busy, friendly hotel, clearly at the heart of the community. Back in Lincolnshire I raved about The George at Stamford. Clearly that place values its heritage, but perhaps its owners also see the hotel as a tourist attraction in its own right. There's none of that self-consciousness at The Golden Lion, just a stream of people passing through with the help of cheerful staff. Something about it screams "lazy Sunday" at me. So I spontaneously award myself a half-day off and decide to stay the night. My bike gets locked away next to the boiler, the pannier gets dumped in the room and it's straight to the Sunday roast – which is perhaps even better than the man in Topcliffe had predicted.

Once run by the now defunct hotel chain Trust House Forte, The Golden Lion was taken over by George and Greta Crow in 1998. Difficult as it is to believe, the couple had no experience of hotels, having previously made a living in the world of travelling fairgrounds. But with three young children to look after, they were keen to put down roots. More than 20 years on, the hotel has flourished under genuinely local ownership. And now, two of those three children are running the place. Daughters Allanda and Scarlett are joint managers, although one gets the impression that both Mum and Dad put a hand on the tiller from time to time.

I sit down opposite Allanda on a leather sofa in a timeless bar directly overlooking the Great North Road. My view is dominated by fireplaces and wooden doors with polished brass handles. I know they're polished because I've already seen the lady out with the Brasso. Tradition runs through this place like a stick of rock.

"Northallerton is a market town and we're a really important part of it," she says, in a soft North Yorkshire accent that, to my Southern ear, has hints of Teesside in it too. "You could almost say we're the heart and soul of the place. So what we do, well it's got to be in keeping with its history. We keep updating things of course. But," and here she gives an involuntary shudder, "we just couldn't do super-modern."

Please don't. The fabric of the building dates back to 1730, but the old well shaft, glassed over in the bar, is taken as evidence of an older building on the same site. In the coaching days there was enough stabling for 75 horses – indeed some of the buildings survive to the rear.

"Horses on the ground floor, stable hands directly above," advises history-loving Dee on reception.

During the Second World War it was well-used by aircrew based at nearby RAF Leeming. Among them, No 427 (Lion) squadron from the Royal Canadian Air Force. Some of its crew couldn't believe their luck when they saw the name of the pub. So when Northallerton awoke one day to find its statue missing, it didn't take a genius to work out who might have scaled the building to bag a new mascot. We're told that after the police made "an urgent but discreet call", the lion reappeared. It's stayed there ever since.

In the afternoon I take to Waterstones for a browse in the bookshop's local history section. But even that feels wrong – much as Dave and Sue's living room felt wrong in Lincolnshire. It's what I do in my "normal" life, not this nomadic one. Still, I now have enough Ordnance Surveys to take me well into Northumberland. Delaying gratification, I wait till I've secured one of the Golden Lion's many sofas before lovingly un-concertina-ing them. I do feel sorry for people who don't understand that a map is there to be read just as much as a novel.

Later still, I wander up the high street – to find that Civil War characters continue to stalk me. The Porch House, now a B&B, is the oldest property in town. According to local legend it was visited twice by King Charles I – once as a guest in 1640 and then again as a prisoner in 1647. This was when the Scots were in the process of selling him back to Parliament, allowing the B&B's website to claim that "it was through the Porch Door that the constitutional monarchy came into being and the absolute monarchy was left behind in history".

I walk a little further and have a quick pint in The Standard pub, a friendly local where everyone greets one another by saying "Now Then" – even when they answer the mobile. There's a happy, beery fuzz about the place, but we're all running out of weekend. Some of us have got to work, others of us have got to push pedals. I down my drink and walk back to my room, from where I can see the shiny mane of the golden lion reflecting the street lamps. I don't feel remotely guilty about that half-day. Northallerton, you've been magnificent.

DAY SEVEN

NORTHALLERTON TO SUNDERLAND BRIDGE

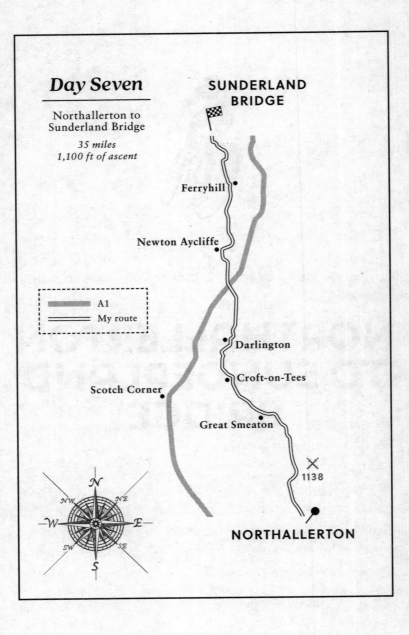

Day Seven

Northallerton to
Sunderland Bridge

35 miles
1,100 ft of ascent

SUNDERLAND
BRIDGE

Ferryhill

Newton Aycliffe

A1
My route

Darlington

Croft-on-Tees

Scotch Corner

Great Smeaton

✕
1138

NORTHALLERTON

N
NW NE
W E
SW SE
S

The good news is that my room directly overlooks the Great North Road. The bad news is that this "artery of a nation" still wakes early. Today the soundtrack is of a squeaky bread trolley being wheeled out of a rackety lorry for Cooplands the Bakers. It is barely 5 a.m. Over the next hour and a half I hear Northallerton wake up in fits and starts: the metallic shudder of shutters unfurling and the insistent warning of reversing klaxons. By the time I come down for breakfast The Golden Lion has forgotten about leisurely Sunday roasts and is gearing up for a business-like Monday. Outside it's cold, the coldest day yet, forcing me to reach for full-length trousers rather than my usual shorts. There's still a northerly, needless to say, but once again there's no rain in the forecast. The details matter hugely. As well as monitoring gradient on the map, I find myself becoming a one-man weather station, obsessively charting temperature as well as both the speed and the direction of the wind.

The bike emerges unscathed from a night in the boiler room and gets wheeled out through the carriage arch. I've got my leaving routine off-pat now. The clunk-click of the pannier getting attached to the frame, the water bottle sliding onto the mount on the down tube and the back bidon getting stuffed with gels and chocolate bars. On with the helmet, off we go. What passes for a rush hour in north Northallerton soon dissolves as the high street morphs into first industrial estates and then open country. This section of road is probably the most dangerous along my whole route – give or take that aberration on the dual carriageway. The temptation is to ride in the gutter – sacrificing my safety for their convenience. Instead, I make myself ride more assertively, slightly more centrally, my position hopefully sending a clear message – don't overtake here, just be patient. As it happens, every driver is perfectly respectful, but it's wearing. Single-carriageway A-roads are just too narrow to allow us to be easy bedfellows. However, in this neck of the woods the map shows few alternatives, so I plough on regardless.

A few miles north of the town, I pull in at a lay-by where an obelisk marks another Great North Road battle. While all the previous ones have essentially been between monarch and rebels, the Battle of the Standard introduces a new feature – marauding Scots. In fact it's almost compulsory for Scots to be described as marauding in any battle-related literature in the North of England. On this occasion under

King David I, they had crossed the River Tweed in March 1138 and devastated parts of the country with what the information panel here calls "vicious savagery". King Stephen was otherwise engaged with a rebellion in the south, so Thurstan, the ageing Archbishop of York, was sent north to get a grip.

Across the high ground to the east, Thurstan arranged for a series of banners to be raised on top of a crude carriage. The flags represented the great Northern saints: St Cuthbert of Durham, St Peter of York, St John of Beverley and St Wilfred of Ripon. This was the standard that gave the battle its name. Thurstan didn't take command in the field, but he did set the tone of it, exhorting the English to fight in God's name against "an army more barbarous than any race of pagans". They were greatly outnumbered, but better led and better armed. After a row over tactics, King David I had put 6,000 Galloway Picts in the front line. The panel board continues:

"They had a reputation for ferocity and courage but were lightly armed and clad in short kilts leaving their buttocks half-naked."

Baring buttocks in March was never going to end well. The English held firm and eventually broke through the Scottish line, killing many thousands but somehow allowing many more to escape in good order. There are no Bloody Oaks nor a Bloody Meadow, but to the south there is both a Red Hill and a Scots Pit Lane. Legend has it that the latter was the site of a mass grave. However, details are sketchy and its precise location hides an inconvenient truth – it lies to the south of the battle site, when one would have thought the Scots would have fallen to the north. Historians argue over whether this means we've got the location wrong or whether the fog of war (literal on this occasion) meant the two sides somehow pivoted so that each faced the wrong way. My travelling companion writes:

> *Standing amid the heathy tussocks of Standard Hill, looking over the Moor, the wide-spreading hill and dale of the Yorkshire landscape fades into a blue or misty distance, and must in its solitude look much the same as it did in those far distant days,*

Well, the land looks a little more cultivated and of course the road is rarely empty of traffic, but yes, a century on everything else is much as Harper found it.

About half a mile further on, my south-north route is bisected by another heading west-east. For me it's a pretty nondescript stretch – the odd farmhouse, one curiously placed car repair garage. In between, even regular drivers probably never notice the first footpath heading across the fields from Danby Wiske, let alone the second heading in the opposite direction across the greenest of meadows a few hundred yards further on. But thanks to the author Alfred Wainwright, they form part of one of the most famous long-distance trails in the country – the Coast to Coast Walk. Wainwright is most famous for his idiosyncratic guides to the fells of the Lake District, but in the early 1970s he dreamt up the idea of a walk across northern England. His brainchild starts at St Bees Head in Cumbria and ends at Robin Hood's Bay in North Yorkshire – about 190 miles in all. Walkers are meant to dip their boots in the sea at either end to prove the point. In between they cross three national parks – the Lake District, the Yorkshire Dales and the North York Moors. Take a look at the gradient profile and this stretch is a blessed relief; gentle descents from Reeth down to Richmond followed by nothing too strenuous toward Osmotherley and Kirkby in Cleveland. But Wainwright had an instinctive dislike of flat country, so the Vale of Mowbray in general and Danby in particular, got short shrift:

Danby Wiske was a sore disappointment. It was an attractive little community but had not the charm I expected and all I could get to eat was a bag of crisps. At only 110 feet above sea level, Danby is the lowest point on the journey between the coastal extremities; to me it was a veritable Slough of Despond.

The locals have sensibly ignored the insult and concentrated on catering for a regular stream of rucksack-bearing visitors. There are more modern brick-built houses than I'd have expected in this part of the world – and still no shop.

But perhaps there doesn't need to be when The White Swan sells sun cream, paracetamol, plasters and chocolate bars along with the more usual fare. The barman reckons that the pub wouldn't be viable without the walkers, although he disputes the numbers.

"You hear figures of fifteen thousand walkers a year bandied about," he tells me. "Absolute rubbish. They all have to walk past here and in a twenty-week season that would mean seven hundred and fifty a week, so about a hundred a day. We don't get anywhere near that number."

But there's a steady stream, alright – and that's despite the fact that it's not an officially designated National Trail. The big surprise for me was the number of foreign walkers. Here, they reckon that the international league table would be led by Australians, followed by Americans, Dutch, Canadians and New Zealanders. Wainwright's guides to the fells were a largely British phenomenon; his Coast to Coast Walk has gone global.

I meet Dennis Smith and his wife Mariam Morgan-Smith, an American couple who have just completed Day 11 of 16. But why are they here in the first place?

"We sat in our local restaurant in Albuquerque for our thirty-ninth wedding anniversary last year and I said let's do something more exciting next year," says Mariam with a smile.

Over the last 11 days "more exciting" has involved torrential rain on the Lake District fells where the paths became impromptu rivers. But aren't there low routes too, alternative paths avoiding the peaks?

"Even the low routes are high," says Dennis with feeling. "Even the low routes had us beat."

"So are you enjoying it?"

Dennis puffs out his cheeks for just a couple of seconds.

"We're enjoying the victory at the end of the day," he says, happy with this precise formulation of words.

"You mean it's tougher than you thought?"

"Much tougher."

"Any injuries?"

"His ankle. My knee," adds Mariam.

"But you're going to make it?"

"We'll make it."

I'm sure they will. Despite the adversity, the Smiths are clearly revelling in the challenge and enjoying a slice of un-touristy England in the process. It has been a pleasure to meet them.

Back on the road, it's quiet till Great Smeaton where I take refuge from the wind in the parish church. Bike rides and churches go together for me. The regular rhythm of the road punctuated by a musty contemplation. In smaller villages like this – as well as the ones I more often roam around in Norfolk – they are often the only public building. Philip Larkin's poem *Church Going* sums up my feelings entirely and uncannily. At a loss with many of the architectural definitions, unsure about faith and yet drawn inexorably to sacred buildings. Here, I discover that the church is the only one in this country to be dedicated to St Eloy – although there are many more in his native France. He's the patron saint of blacksmiths. And, whether by coincidence or not, the collection of buildings immediately next to the church once formed The Blacksmith's Arms, where mail coaches made their one change of horses between Northallerton and Darlington. The nineteenth-century author Tom Bradley, mentioned previously on Day Five of my ride, tells a story in his book *The Old Coaching Days in Yorkshire* about the ruthless coachman Ralph Soulsby, who worked on the *Wellington* – a service which ran between Newcastle and London:

"It is on record that once during a period when the *Wellington* was running in opposition [in effect racing] he succeeded in killing three out of his four horses on the short stage from Great Smeaton to Northallerton... Opposition coaches were terribly hard on horseflesh; they used to gallop every inch of the road, up hill and down dale and Soulsby's third horse dropped dead just opposite the church and he finished his journey to the Golden Lion with but a single horse."

———

Every so often I notice that the wind isn't quite so much in my face. And I'm now so in tune with both bike and weather that I can clock the precise moment – on a left-hander at Low Entercommon – when the front wheel decisively cuts through the northerly, like a sailor completing a tack. It's not that the wind is now in my sails, it's just no longer actively hindering me. Utterly inconsequential to the rest of the world, but – after 250-odd miles – a huge moment for me.

County Durham is now very close as the crow flies, because a long, lazy loop of the River Tees dangles south, enclosing a sliver of land known as the Sockburn Peninsula. The landscape and the place names are now becoming more familiar. My first job was as a trainee reporter on the *Darlington and Stockton Times*. My starting salary in 1991 was £6,000 – down from £7,200 because I had failed my shorthand exam. Like the rest of the junior reporters, I got to cover Darlington Magistrates' Court, agricultural shows across the entire Yorkshire Dales and parish council meetings in the likes of Middleton St George and Hurworth on Tees – the latter now very close. Frustratingly, I can recall less than I'd imagined; it's only as the views appear in front of me that my memory is jogged – a good story here, the place where I crashed my Mini there.

As I cycle into the village of Croft, the Tees sidles up on my right shoulder. Until now it's lain hidden behind thickets of trees and large houses – presumably with extensive riverside gardens. The Tees, like the Trent, feels like one of those Big Boundaries. Cross it and I'm not just leaving Croft for Hurworth. I'm also swapping Yorkshire for the North East of England. Yorkshire, though, is going out on a high. First there's the Georgian elegance of The Croft Hotel, built in 1835 to help tourists enjoy the nearby Croft Spa whose waters had become very fashionable.

Not that they found favour with Harper:

> It behoves me to speak respectfully of Croft and its Spa, for its waters are as nasty as those of Harrogate, with that flavour of rotten eggs so highly approved by the medical profession, and only the vagaries of fashion can be held accountable for the comparative neglect of the one and the favouring of the other... Sulphur renders both equally nauseous and healthful, but Croft finds few votaries compared with its great and successful rival, and a gentle melancholy marks the spot...

Then there's a rectory made famous by Lewis Carroll, the author of *Alice in Wonderland*. His father moved here in 1843 when Lewis was 11 years old. One of its top-floor windows has mirror-image graffiti which is said to have inspired *Alice Through the Looking Glass*. Carroll's father's old church lies directly opposite. St Peter's demands to be visited, not least for another shaft of literary light – the wide smile of the Cheshire Cat is said to be based on a gargoyle-type feature at the end of a fourteenth-century stone chair inside. But, sadly, Croft joins Scrooby, Austerfield and North Otterington on my list of churches with locked doors. In fact, apart from a mention on the village sign, Croft steadfastly refuses to jump on the *Alice* bandwagon. I can't work out whether to admire their English reserve or berate them for a lack of entrepreneurship.

———

Back on the modern A1, drivers are approaching a landmark to which the signposts have been counting down for 40 miles. Newcastle might be the regional capital, Durham is a World Heritage Site, but the ancient code of A1 sign-writers decrees that Scotch Corner must take precedence. For a glorified roundabout it has a very high profile, but then this junction has been pivotal since Roman times, particularly for travellers heading to Scotland. Those aiming for Edinburgh and the east coast stuck to Dere Street, those going to Glasgow and the west joined what is now the A66. Penrith lies 50 lonely miles across the Pennines.

For me, the aura of Scotch Corner is tempting but ultimately resistible. Instead, I cross into County Durham via the medieval bridge at Croft and head across the flood meadows on the old road toward Darlington. A boy racer deliberately leaves just millimetres to spare as he overtakes me at speed, the worst incident I've experienced since the sweary lorry driver on Islington's Upper Street. Welcome to the North East.

All I'm focused on is finding the town centre and a bike shop because I have discovered that after seven days on the road my backside is in desperate need of a special kind of cream. Chamois cream is so-called because, back in the

1940s, the earliest specialist cycling shorts included a leather pad made from the skin of the chamois – a goat/antelope cross native to the mountain slopes of Europe. The first incarnation of the cream was designed for the leather itself – to keep it supple. We don't use its skin any more and these days the cream goes directly on our own hide, but the old name has stuck. And I've urgently needed some "shammy cream" since yesterday afternoon. The first two shops can't help, but I strike gold at The Iron Horse Cyclery. I hand over my money, take the bottle and linger for a second too long at the counter. The assistant reads me like a book.

"Would you like somewhere to, err… apply it?"

For some reason the word "apply" has greater resonance with a North East accent.

"Do you know what? That would be great."

"Just pop upstairs, don't worry there's no cameras or anything."

Cameras? I hadn't thought of that. So, on the first floor of a converted warehouse in Clark's Yard, next to a line of pink toddler bikes, I find myself squatting down, dropping my pants and slathering a generous portion of white, sticky stuff across my nether parts. Mustering as much dignity as possible, I return downstairs.

"Thanks so much, I really needed that."

"No bother, all part of the service."

Once again I've been a rank amateur. Anyone will tell you that long periods on the bike plays havoc down below –

and that prevention is better than cure. I've never had a problem before, but then again I've never ridden for seven consecutive days. In Lincolnshire I neglected my stomach and paid the penalty. Until County Durham, I've been neglecting my backside. The £13.99 for my Ozone Elite Chamois Cream was money well spent.

Food-wise, I'm discovering that Full English breakfasts tend to go down pretty well at lunchtime. And my meal upstairs at Darlington's atmospheric Covered Market is the best yet. Before the bacon arrives I tuck into a surprisingly complimentary – if patronising – Harper.

> Darlington, to which we now come, is a very busy, very prosperous, very much rebuilt town, nursing a sub-Metropolitan swagger of architectural pretension in its chief streets infinitely unlike anything expected by the untravelled in these latitudes... There is a distinctly Holloway Road-plus-Whitechapel Road-and-Kennington Lane air about Darlington, which does but add to the piquancy of those streets... It is a town only now beginning to realise that prosperity must make some outward show of the fact, and it is accordingly going in for show in whole-hearted fashion.

I spend a happy hour exploring old haunts. Darlington calls its streets "rows" and "gates" and they have pleasingly medieval names: Skinnergate, Houndgate, Prebend Row and

High Row. The newspaper was based in Priestgate and I pass the window of the office where I eventually passed my crucial 100-words-per-minute shorthand exam – but only with the help of an exceptionally generous interpretation of the rules from the kindliest of editor's secretaries. Thank you, Doreen.

Memories of stories past now come flooding back, including meeting an up-and-coming Tony Blair at a homelessness protest – on High Row. As the MP of a neighbouring constituency, the future Prime Minister was a young man in a hurry in every sense and it was very much a grabbed interview. My main memory is that on a windswept day he was more worried about how his hair looked for the photo than the questions I was asking or the answers he was giving. In contrast Alan Milburn, the equally ambitious MP for Darlington, always had time for us, whatever the weather. From politicians to army veterans, and from grieving widows to celebrating centenarians, we spoke to them all. And there is something quite surreal about returning to the place where you learned your trade after a quarter of a century. Looking back now, my main feeling is gratitude for the patience of the people in the face of occasionally naive or downright ignorant questions from us pesky cub reporters.

In the North East, it's less easy to valley hop in the way one can in Hertfordshire or Bedfordshire. Heading north from Darlington I climb first Harrowgate Hill and then Beaumont Hill en route to Newton Aycliffe. The busy A167 becomes tiresome too, so I attempt a short cut – or at least a "quiet cut" – through an industrial estate, but only succeed in getting lost around the massive Gestamp car parts plant. In compensation, the new town of Aycliffe shows off its town planning features with leafy avenues and decent bike paths. If twinning northern towns with southern counterparts was a fashionable thing to do, Stevenage would fit the bill nicely.

Central Avenue wends its way back to Rushyford and finds the Great North Road gearing up for its greatest challenge yet – a sizeable hill of magnesian limestone set four-square across its path at Ferryhill. The escarpment lies 180 metres above sea level in places and presented the old mail coaches with a terrific obstacle. The problem was a classic challenge for an entrepreneurial turnpike trust: raise enough money to dig out a cutting and charge a toll to the passengers who benefitted. Such schemes had worked across the country for decades, but when the Boroughbridge, Darlington and Durham Turnpike started work in 1832, its investors had one factor against them – timing. The railways were beginning their inexorable march across the country. Like a retail company investing in bricks-and-mortar shops when everyone's flocking to glitzy websites, the turnpike's business model was about to become irredeemably broken. After much agonising, its directors abandoned the project in 1835, leaving a scar across the landscape for generations. It wouldn't be until after the First World War that publicly funded Durham County Council finished work started by private speculators.

I set up on the middle chain ring and resign myself to a slow grind on the older and steeper road. Terraced houses climb the hill, red brick by red brick. At the summit, a quick left turn sees me on a bridge across the cutting where the turnpike road is surprisingly far below. The last time I've had a view like this was at a breezy Archway in London, where I could look back at the gleaming City of London. Six days later that northerly wind is still man-to-man marking me, once again channelled by a navvy-built gorge. To the south the fields of County Durham are framed by metal footbridges slung across what locals call "The Cut". To the north the immediate landscape looks benign enough – more rolling fields criss-crossed by electricity pylons. But in the distance, larger peaks loom.

Ferryhill town centre is perched on the ridge and the Dean and Chapter pub immediately takes my eye. The name is a reminder that Durham Cathedral was the big landowner here, but the pub remembers the colliery of the same name, sunk further down the hill in the early years of the twentieth century. If I cross the bridge I'm in the suburb of Dean Bank, purpose-built to house the pit's miners. The architecture is certainly all of a piece from the school to the magnificent Literary Institute building – which, unbelievably, had to be saved from demolition at the turn of this century. Most of the streets are named after famous engineers: Newcomen, Newton, Bessemer and Brunel. And behind Davy Street, I find the most "professional" set of allotments I have ever seen – almost as much greenhouse and polytunnel as produce in the ground. And, at the far end, old pigeon lofts looking north to the open sky.

Returning to the town centre I have a closer look at the pub. An inscription says it's dedicated to the 73 miners who lost their lives at the pit over the years. Back in South Yorkshire – in my ignorance – I'd seen the disasters at Bentley as isolated incidents, but it's becoming clear that they were much more regular than that. Whether they died singly or in larger numbers, death underground was an occupational hazard.

I need to know more. And it turns out that the place to go is the Durham Mining Museum down the road in Spennymoor. Occupying a few small rooms on the first floor of Spennymoor Town Hall, the museum appears at first sight to take the traditional approach to curating. They've festooned every wall with as many artefacts as you can get your hands on: lamps, helmets, photos, maps, banners; even a satisfyingly large chunk of the mineral pyrite. But look closer and it's doing something more significant too. Volunteers here have painstakingly catalogued the deaths of 24,800 miners across northern England – 15,000 of them in County Durham alone. Go online and the human cost is expressed in a different form, depending on when you visit. For the month of May it records ten different disasters across the north over the years at a cumulative cost of more than 500 lives. The "accidents" were a sorry mix of explosions, flooding, fire and falls.

The staff here know their stuff. Many's the time a visitor drops in to ask about a relative who, family legend has it, died down a certain pit in a certain era. The exhaustive records mean this museum is as likely as anywhere in the country to be able to provide an authoritative answer. It has copies of all the disaster reports too. It turns out that the Bentley incident of 1978 was the third but last of its kind in the UK. The inspector forensically examines why seven men were killed underground when a "man-riding train" carrying 65 people ran out of control so disastrously. Two people with similar surnames had been mixed up, so that one was given a job for which he hadn't been trained. The gradient of the railway was too steep, the signalling lights weren't working, the brakes were deficient, maintenance staff had been diverted to different jobs, the guard wasn't in place and the driver had been in the wrong gear. A catalogue of errors and system failures that led to Robert Aitcheson, Donald Box, Kenneth Green, David R. Hall, Geoffrey Henderson, Michael Edward Hickman and James Mitchell losing their lives. Even as recently as 1978 it feels as if miners' lives were held very cheap.

———

Back on my journey, the Great North Road is continuing to weave its economic magic. A few years ago Thinford was little more than a small community around a roundabout, but now it's home to Durhamgate, a £100 million "mixed-use regeneration scheme" complete with campus-style offices, housing and cafés. While somewhere like Spennymoor – off the main drag – can feel slightly down-at-heel, Thinford is becoming a hi-tech gateway to the cathedral city of Durham. Location still matters.

From there, it's pretty much all downhill to my hotel at the hamlet of Sunderland Bridge – so-called despite it being nowhere near the city of Sunderland. The original bridge looks as if it's been here for centuries – a peaceful spot to look down upon the River Wear which is roughly midway through its 60-mile journey from the eastern Pennines to the sea.

Each day I've been posting updates online for friends back home. One exiled North-Easterner had berated me for declaring that I'd made it to the north when I crossed the Trent. He now needs to know that I have crossed his own river – if only to shut him up. I punch out a few words, select a photo and then take a long look upstream. Mackem John, I decide, does have a point. I can't put my finger on it, but it's clear that the landscape has turned wilder by degrees.

As I get up to go, a notification comes through on the phone. John hasn't replied to my post as such, but I have got a tiny "thumbs up". It means nothing and it means everything. It means I am now definitively, categorically and unquestionably... up North.

DAY EIGHT

SUNDERLAND BRIDGE TO CRAMLINGTON

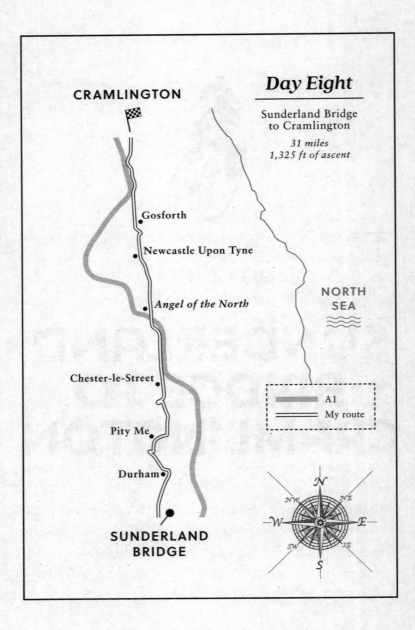

CRAMLINGTON

Day Eight

Sunderland Bridge
to Cramlington

*31 miles
1,325 ft of ascent*

• Gosforth

• Newcastle Upon Tyne

Angel of the North

NORTH
SEA

Chester-le-Street •

A1
My route

Pity Me •

Durham •

SUNDERLAND
BRIDGE

The city of Durham now lies tantalisingly close and everyone staying at The Honest Lawyer seems to be heading in that direction. Many look suspiciously like proud parents about to bestow restaurant-quality meals upon underfed and undergraduate sons and daughters. I'm certainly the only one on a bike. Black pudding with your breakfast, sir? Well, to be honest I reckon I'm the one person who can justify the calories. Something makes me want to return to the Wear before I get the bike out. The tall Croxdale Viaduct takes the East Coast Main Line across the river to the west, while the modern road eases past to the east. The original Sunderland Bridge has a more human scale, allowing me to look down on the boulders breaking the water's flow, the spume bright-white in the morning sun. I take a deep draught of northern air. It's good to measure my progress from an ancient bridge spanning a timeless river. And of course it's another opportunity to appreciate that all I've got to do today is cycle from A to B.

I start pedalling. This part of County Durham used to be a nightmare for coach drivers. A sharp turn to get onto Sunderland Bridge had been identified as an accident blackspot after an incident in 1815. Six years later, two passengers died when they were flung over the bridge from the outside seats of a mail. Eye-witnesses told how the coach driver James Auld had whipped the horses too hard and taken the bend too fast. According to the writer Samuel Tuke Richardson in his c.1890 book *Family Annals By Road and Rail By Flood and Field*, Auld was later found guilty of manslaughter for "driving furiously and unlawfully". Auld subsequently insisted that he too went flying over the bridge's parapet and only survived because he hung onto his reins, waiting to be rescued. Admittedly our main source for that aspect of the tale is Auld's alcoholic son who spoke to Richardson in Darlington some years later. "He repeated the story," recorded the writer, "while weeping copiously on my bosom in Blackwellgate."

Having crossed the Wear at Sunderland Bridge, the coachmen crested one more hill to find the same river in front of them at Durham. The Wear is one of the Pennine rivers *not* to get the memo about heading west/east, putting in some stubborn northern twists in this neck of the woods. But this last hill allows me to freewheel down to the suburb of Old Elvet, where Durham University is busy spending millions on new buildings – including the Bill Bryson Library, I notice. Harper, writing at the turn of the last century, and feeling rather grumpy at this juncture, wouldn't have recognised it:

> *Besides being dirty and shabby it is endowed with a cobble-stoned road which, as if its native unevenness were not sufficient, may generally be found strewed with fragments of hoop-iron, clinkers and other puncturing substances calculated to give tragical pauses to the exploring cyclist who essays to follow the route whose story is set out in these pages.*

There were plenty of tragical pauses for car drivers as the twentieth century wore on, simply because the medieval bridges couldn't handle the volume of modern traffic. Durham Cathedral is built on a tight loop which means that the Wear has to be crossed twice more. The 1960s Millburngate Bridge and the 1970s New Elvet Bridge have partially relieved the pressure, leaving the originals free for pedestrians and cyclists.

Crossing Old Elvet Bridge plunges me into the heart of the city, which instantly screams "World Heritage Site" by the sheer number of international tourists and food outlets. After hundreds of miles of "normal" England, it's quite a culture shock.

For a start it's noisy – not least because my later start means that the tourists have arrived. A large block of flats is going up alongside the river. The builders' drills in the distance compete with the chatter of different languages on the streets. An attention-seeking busker tries to belt out "Hey Jude" above the hubbub. Nothing remotely unreasonable, but nevertheless an assault on my senses compared to previous days. I start by climbing Saddler Street, colonised by every restaurant chain you've ever heard of and some you perhaps haven't. I'm now approaching the centre of this near-island, where some sort of elemental force seems to drag all of us visitors up the hill.

The legend of Durham centres around St Cuthbert who died on Lindisfarne Island – some 80 miles further north – in 687. When it later came under threat from the Danes, the monks fled, taking Cuthbert's remains with them. After seven years of wandering they first settled at Chester-le-Street before moving to Ripon in North Yorkshire. It's when the monks were meant to be returning to Chester-le-Street in the late tenth century that they diverted here. The legend says that the cart carrying the coffin suddenly stopped after their bishop had a vision of Cuthbert demanding to be taken to "Dunholme". No one had heard of the place, but then a girl walked by and asked a woman if she had seen a lost cow. The woman said she had seen the beast heading toward Dunholme. The monks duly followed her to this impressive peninsula, where steep gorges provided natural defences against any foe. The remains of St Cuthbert have lain largely undisturbed ever since.

The road gets steeper, narrower and consequentially darker. I'm walking with the bike, but the tyres still judder along the cobbles of Owengate. Slowly the shape of the cathedral reveals itself – first the two western towers, then the rest of this exceptional building along the far side of a closely mown green. Initially I take this as the classic cathedral close. But once I've reached the plateau I realise that Durham takes it one stage further with a castle – now part of the university – sharing the high ground. Living near Norwich, I'm used to the tranquillity of such a close. This one feels different. Between cathedral and green a dozen film wagons form a community to themselves, protected by guards in day-glow orange. Students intermingle with us tourists and, off to the left, a group of Deliveroo riders are being raucously slapstick.

Inside, the monumental carved Norman pillars along the nave feel heavy and dark, recalling Sir Walter Scott's line about it being "half Church of God, half castle 'gainst the Scot". Unusually, I don't linger. I tell myself that's because I'm concerned for the security of the bike, locked around a drainpipe, but in reality it's because this solitary me feels slightly less comfortable amid the gaggles of people – even gaggles partially hushed by the majesty of a holy place. Time instead to take in the wider landscape around Palace Green. Fair play to the visionary bishop, and indeed the wandering cow – it's a spectacular spot with learned university buildings completing the perimeter. My only disappointment is that the fringes of this "summit" are so wooded that I can't quite make out the Wear below.

————

Cycling back down the hill doesn't feel quite right here. So I compromise, scooting down with a foot on just one pedal ready to jump off if pedestrian traffic gets too heavy. I find the market place, home to the town hall and a ridiculously large statue of the third Marquis of Londonderry – a military man turned coal mine baron from the Victorian era. I then pick up the route the coaches would have taken along Silver Street to the second crossing of the Wear at Framwellgate Bridge. Once you cross, it's as if the supply of tourists has been abruptly switched off. Here on North Road, Durham feels normal, down-at-heel even. Of course all towns and cities have that slightly more run-down street, the one that's home to the vape stores and the takeaways, but here the contrast seems particularly acute. It's almost as if the natives have fought a losing battle for their own city and have retreated to the north of the river, determined to make one last stand around the bus station.

For me, the only way is up. Seriously up. I head under the viaduct which keeps the East Coast Main Line out of trouble and continue to climb. Yesterday I would have found it a real struggle, but today I feel as if I could conquer Alpe d'Huez without a problem. Has my body finally adapted to life on the road or is it just one of those days? The Durham of tourists gives way to the County Durham of former pit villages. I move from North Road to Front Street somewhere between Framwellgate Moor and the curiously named Pity Me – I'm starting to discover that you can traverse most of County Durham without leaving North Roads and Front Streets. There were four pits in this area, Brasside, Framwellgate, Dryburn and Frankland. All were closed before the outbreak of the Second World War, yet all these years on, the lie of the land and the cut of the houses somehow give the game away.

The A167 is about to become a dual carriageway, so I veer east, narrowly avoiding a sewage works with the wonderful postal address of "Stank Lane, Pity Me". Soon I find myself on a country lane, but is it the right road? Three MAMILs are speeding along in the opposite direction, but come to a halt when I hail them. They politely reassure me that I'm heading the correct way, but as they head off, one mutters to the other "Well, that's another segment buggered." Across the country cyclists use the Strava app to sub-divide every road into "segments" like this. On balance, trying to be the rider with the fastest time along a particular stretch is pretty harmless fun, but sometimes, just sometimes…

Then it's Chester-le-Street, Barley Mow and Birtley in quick succession as I realise that I've come within the gravitational pull of a greater Tyneside. That country lane will prove to be the last for a while. But cycling continues to be easy. There's plenty of traffic, but there's invariably a bike lane too.

The A1 lies to the east. Norman Webster, whose 1974 book *The Great North Road* beautifully captures the years when the road was being rapidly upgraded, called it "a magnificent modern highway of bold embankments and wide cuttings which avoids the ugliness of the former scenes and captures the best of the Durham greenery." The old road and the new meet at Junction 66 amid much swooping of spur roads. I negotiate those before being confronted with the massive Angel of the North – out of nowhere. You wouldn't think a celestial being with a 54-metre wingspan could hide in the landscape, but from the south Antony Gormley's sculpture does just that. Built on the site of pit-head colliery baths, it was quickly taken to the hearts of North Easterners after being unveiled in 1998.

Gormley had initially been resistant to the wooing of Gateshead Council; as he recalled in 2018 for North-East newspaper the *Evening Chronicle*, he had told the council sharply that "I don't do sculptures for motorways". But the road wasn't really the point. The council wanted a statement piece – something acknowledging the past, but looking to the future. And once Gormley had visited, he was converted by the lofty location and mining heritage – even comparing it to an Iron Age tumulus.

He took the commission and then set out to immerse himself in the region, taking inspiration from the shipbuilders of the Tyne as well as those who had once earned their living underground, indeed under *this* ground.

"The Angel resists our post-industrial amnesia and bears witness to the hundreds and thousands of colliery workers who had spent the last three hundred years mining coal beneath the surface," he wrote.

Post-industrial amnesia! While I couldn't give it a name, that's exactly the feeling I'd been unable to articulate back at Bentley in Yorkshire where an anonymous "community woodland" struggled to do justice to the pit buildings it had both replaced and erased.

On this windswept bluff overlooking the Team Valley, the Angel took some anchoring. Its foundations are sunk 20-metres deep into the solid rock below. To counter the wind, its wings are tilted slightly inwards – providing a literal protection from the elements and a figurative embrace to the 90,000 drivers who pass by every day.

"It's a real symbol of the area," says the lady serving drinks at the Coffee Station kiosk. "I mean, we've got lots of them up here, we've got the Tyne Bridge, the Sage, Penshaw Monument, there's loads. But this is the one you'll see on the TV."

I hang around longer than I mean to among a group of visitors doing just the same. And they're not just long-distance ones; three cyclists from Whitley Bay are busy with the selfies too.

The cost of this masterpiece was £800,000. I cycle out of the car park and take one last look over my shoulder. Less than a million pounds... what a complete bargain.

Birtley has become Low Fell which soon becomes Gateshead – and the beautifully smooth bike paths get better and better. As a cyclist I haven't been treated this well since Stevenage. From Gateshead the contours start to dip drastically toward the Tyne along steep streets that mail coach passengers used to hate. But since those distant days the engineers have thrown spectacular high-level bridges across the Tyne valley, saving several hundred feet of descent and ascent in the process.

I think it was this vista which helped me fall instantly in love with Newcastle when I first came here in 1986 for an interview at the university. Arriving by train from the south, you can't help but be affected by the majesty of the river and the multiplicity of its bridges. There's no drifting in through faceless suburbs, just one "wow" moment – unmatched by any other city in England. The university was good enough to offer me a place, I ended up living in the North East for eight years and I have trusted my first impressions of cities ever since. So, in a rather self-absorbed way that I had better not bang on about, cycling over the coat hanger-shaped Tyne Bridge brings a lump to the throat. To begin with I'm even a little nervous that the older me won't feel the same as the 19-year-old version, but, thankfully, it still takes my breath away. The traffic is incessant, the pollution is probably terrible, but the view is magnificent. Beneath us, the merchants' houses along Quayside; above, the tall spire of the Georgian All Saints Church, before more distant impressions of vigorous retail and commerce. A patch of lime green amid the chimney pots is gradually revealed to be a tiny astroturf roof garden complete with recliners and pot plants. I take endless photos of the bridge, the bike, the city and the river – none of which quite capture the magic of the moment. No doubt the fact that I'm arriving under my own steam is providing its own invisible filter.

To understand Newcastle, you need to know that the city has grown up from the river over the centuries, giving it a multi-layered charm explained beautifully by the architectural critic Ian Nairn:

"It is built on one side of a hundred-foot gorge," he wrote in his 1967 book, *Nairn's Towns*. "And the medieval town struggled up it from the quayside, producing dozens of sets of steps or 'chares' which even in their present neglect can produce a kind of topographical ecstasy as you go up and down, perpetually seeing the same objects in a different way."

Nairn was a maverick who railed against the homogenisation of British architecture in the decades after the war. He coined the phrase "subtopia" to describe the depressing tendency of city hinterlands to lose their identities. Nairn loved Newcastle. Heading up from the quayside, he soon found the neo-classical Grainger Street and Grey Street, roads which he felt ennobled those who walked along them:

"I mean this literally: there are some places that seem to have the gift of transferring or sharing their qualities with the viewer... The precise quality is grandeur without pomposity; everything serious, but not lugubrious, everything formal and firmly urbane but not oppressive."

Hear, hear.

I finally get off the bridge but immediately waste all of its engineering effort by dropping down to the Quayside and enjoying a coffee in the sunshine. From here I sit at the foot of Nairn's gorge with a view of three great bridges. Directly opposite is the unsung Swing Bridge. Built between 1868 and 1876, it sits on a central pontoon and replaced the last in a series of traditional stone bridges, which had done the job for road vehicles but were now starting to inhibit river traffic. The Swing Bridge can turn on its own axis and rest on the pontoon, allowing large ships to come and go on either side. To my right I can see the High Level Bridge – a double-decker carrying both road and rail traffic – the first bridge in the world to do so. And peeking out from behind The Guildhall I can also make out the Newcastle end of the Tyne Bridge, opened much later in 1928. At the time this was the world's longest single-span bridge – and you can imagine the local pride that generated. Almost a century later it remains genuinely iconic. I drink up, get back on the bike and cycle beneath it, feeling rather puny in its substantial shadow.

Downriver from here, my memories from the 1980s are of a riverside that rapidly grew scruffy and neglected. For a student, a floating nightclub called the Tuxedo Princess was about the classiest attraction. It's long gone. Instead there's a bewildering array of newness in brick, glass and tarmac that leaves me disorientated. The Gateshead bank is dominated by the shiny Sage building, a performing arts centre. Further down, the Millennium Bridge puts a twenty-first century spin on the swing bridge idea; with the semi-circular base turning into the air to allow ships to pass through. Apparently the process takes about four and a half minutes. The design is so clever that any litter on the bridge automatically drops into special traps as it rises. Seeing it sitting there, it seems rude not to cycle across. So I break my normal rule about never heading south and head toward another new icon – an old flour mill now transformed into the Baltic Centre for Contemporary Art. The Baltic, the Angel, the Sage and the Millennium Bridge are the four key components of a project to regenerate this area, building a new "NewcastleGateshead" brand in the process. They've done a super job.

I now return to Newcastle across the Swing Bridge, my wheels juddering in the slightest of gaps between the end of the road and the start of the bridge. From this angle you get a much better view of the square keep of the new castle which gave the city its name in Norman times. My route then gets steep rather quickly, particularly along a street called Side. This is the section which would have made the horses labour, a nasty 1:12 gradient which continues up Dean Street and Grey Street. I try to remember Nairn's words, but by bike it's somehow more of a struggle to feel ennobled as I search for a succession of lower gears.

Only two coaching inns are mentioned in the old books. The Queen's Head on Pilgrim Street was the home for the mails while The Turf Hotel on Collingwood Street looked after the stage coaches. The Turf was demolished more than a century ago, while the Queen's Head on Pilgrim Street is now so "restored" into offices that it looks nothing like a pub. Were there others? Harper confidently asserted that none had survived by the time he came calling. Yet these days a pub called The Old George is held up as an example. I eventually find it tucked away in an alley near the Bigg Market. Even the pub's literature can only say that it *might* have been a coaching inn. Yes, there's a courtyard, but that's the only real evidence. I'm going with Harper on this one. If in doubt, go with Harper.

There has to be a bike-friendly way north out of the city centre, but I fail to find it, ending up on a dual carriageway near the university. It's the Great North Road alright, just with rather faster traffic than I would like. Eventually I can lift the bike over some railings onto a pavement next to the vast Town Moor – perhaps one of the biggest open spaces in England so close to a major city. Now I'm off the road, I can start to appreciate it. The approach from the north might not have the wow factor of the Tyne, but it's elegant nevertheless – a non-stop avenue of trees which are starting to come into leaf on this bright May day. Newcastle doesn't suffocate you like some of the bigger northern cities. Its centre is more compact, its outskirts, greener and more accessible. The prosperous suburb of Gosforth arrives remarkably quickly, I thought it was much further north. I'm starting to realise how parochial my old mind-map of Newcastle had been. I covered every inch of the city centre, but I suspect I rarely strayed out of the student suburbs. In any case Gosforth was too well-heeled, it was a place for proper grown-ups who worked at places like Northern Rock and BT.

North of Gosforth the urban sprawl is checked by what the map shows as a solid block of green. As I get closer, this separates out into two golf courses and Newcastle racecourse. Admittedly there are only a few fields before the former mining villages of Wideopen and Seaton Burn. Harper, never a fan of any sort of work being done near his beloved road, lumped them together with Gosforth, saying he was "appalled at the increasing wretchedness and desolation brought by the coal-mining industry upon the scene". I divert onto a footpath to discover a landscape he could but wonder at. Admittedly Wideopen Colliery is still the site of a scrapyard, but beyond it the bigger Weetslade Colliery has become a country park where visitors are invited to look out for grey partridge, otters and kingfishers. I wind my way up to the summit of the old pit heap where three monumental drill bits point skywards – a memorial to the old days. I get chatting to a mountain biker in his sixties who can remember playing up here as a kid. In fact he knew the different shape of every pit heap between here and Blyth, "so that you always knew where you were just by looking at them". Now all utterly transformed. As we gaze out, I get my first glimpse of a grey-blue North Sea to the east, while the darker tones of the Cheviot Hills to the north loom impressively large. High and large. At this height, it's blustery and I have to turn the bike "head to wind" to keep it out of trouble. In a clear blue sky, I comment on a skylark twittering bossily overhead. In turn, the mountain biker points out the sections of the hillside which have been fenced off to protect their nesting sites. This place is clearly well-loved. All in all, Weetslade has gone from wretched to wild.

Another path takes me north toward Seaton Burn along the route of a so-called waggonway – one of many which once existed across the northern coalfield. Waggonways – always with a double "g" in the north east – were wooden railroads used by colliery owners to get their coal to either the Tyne or the coast. Huge freight waggons carrying the coal were hauled by a mixture of horse power, ropes and gravity. In the eighteenth century they were the most efficient form of transport available, not least because the topography made canal building impractical. The North East was their heartland – so much so that the rest of the country referred to them as "Tyneside Roads".

In one form or another, waggonways had been around longer than stage coaches. But they share the distinction of falling out of fashion with the rise of conventional railways. From mail coaches, the railway industry would steal the concept of the strict timetable and a sense of glamour. From waggonways they stole the very idea of the rail, the flanged wheel and the accompanying engineering nous. It's no coincidence that the great railway engineer George Stephenson learned his trade and built Blücher, his first steam engine, just five miles from here. At Killingworth Colliery Blücher could haul 30 tons of coal at four miles an hour. Dig a little deeper and you'll find railway firsts are claimed throughout the North East. Based on its use of waggonways, the Tanfield Railway near Gateshead markets itself as the "World's First Railway". The Hetton Colliery Railway was the first to use no animal power whatsoever. And, famously, the Stockton and Darlington Railway was the world's first steam railway to take freight and paying customers.

My path is a northern outpost of a track which looped all the way down to a staithe on the River Tyne. I follow it in the other direction, across the Great North Road to the site of the Seaton Burn colliery – the end of the line. It's far from being a living museum, but old buildings do survive, the history of each one lovingly explained by a succession of information boards and signposts. Seaton Burn is one of many places along my route where local historians have done an impressively thorough job.

After that, I'm almost done. My bed for the night lies one short stretch of dual carriageway away on the outskirts of

Cramlington. Crucially I cross the border between North Tyneside and Northumberland before I get there. I can rest at The Snowy Owl, knowing that I'm now in England's most northerly county – a county with a stunning coastline and steeper hills. What's more, the sun is shining and my own personal northerly has finally given up the ghost. Tomorrow will be my first day without a headwind.

DAY NINE

CRAMLINGTON TO SEAHOUSES

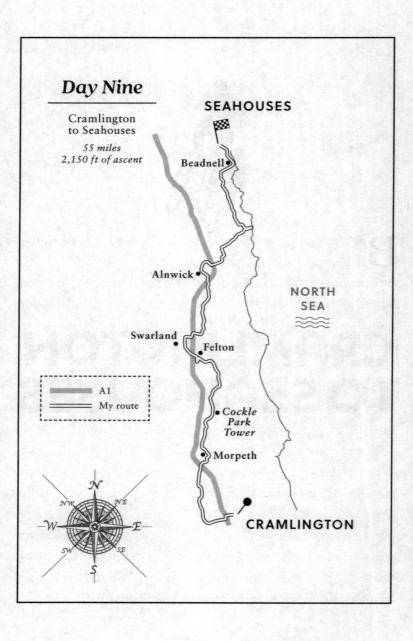

Day Nine

Cramlington
to Seahouses

*55 miles
2,150 ft of ascent*

SEAHOUSES

Beadnell

Alnwick

NORTH
SEA

Swarland

Felton

*Cockle
Park
Tower*

Morpeth

A1
My route

CRAMLINGTON

N
NW   NE
W   E
SW   SE
S

Back home, my usual routine on a Saturday is to tiptoe from the bedroom and get kitted out in the full MAMIL uniform in the spare room. Then it's porridge, garage, bike, helmet, water bottle and cleats. I'll cycle down to the war memorial in the middle of our village for a 6.45 a.m. start. Ex-military man Nige will be there first. He's never been late. Ever. Dave, myself and Jim – last seen at the Indian restaurant in Sawtry – will arrive over the next few minutes with various sorry excuses for our lateness – lost bike lights, late nights or dodgy alarms.

Five years ago none of us made this much effort to exercise. We've yet to work out what sort of sociological earthquake has transformed us – but we're doing it anyway. We don't ride as a peloton, we certainly don't take turns on the front and I suspect none of us will ever join a proper cycling club. Nevertheless we manage to cover 20-odd miles at a half-decent pace, putting the world to rights amid the peace and quiet of the back lanes before someone gets the coffees in at McDonald's.

They were probably fed up with me banging on about this trip, but in the end that hasn't stopped Dave from travelling north to join me for the last three days. The persistent headwind finally switched to a westerly at the very hour he arrived at The Snowy Owl last night. I show him the wind graphics on the weather app. He raises his hands in mock modesty, clearly I should expect nothing less. Side by side, our bikes look like they're made for father and son. My Jamis Aurora in British Racing Green is determinedly old school, his is a black mountain bike with luminous stripes.

We're on the road by 8.30 a.m. and I am instantly reminded that cycling with someone else is a whole different ball game. If I'm chatting I pretty much forget that I'm putting in any effort on the bike. After eight days on my own I really appreciate the difference. While only sporadic, there were moments when it was hard to turn the pedals, times when I concentrated too much on the distance yet to travel rather than the sights yet to see.

From our hotel the A1 is just about within earshot – it's the morning rush hour after all. We cycle toward and then beneath it before being forced into a bit of a diversion around the massive Blagdon Estate. After skirting a typical parkland-style landscape we head north on the quietest of single-track roads. Small birds bustle noisily in the hedgerows, a yellowhammer startles us with its boldness and its brightness on the tarmac and under a blue sky there isn't a car to be seen. Tyneside seems a long way away.

The Blagdon Estate has been in the same family since 1700 – that's 11 generations. Every single owner has been called Matthew, although to be fair there have been some variations. The first three were called Matthew White, the next eight have been called Matthew White Ridley. And over the centuries they've managed to upgrade themselves from plain Mr to Sir and now Viscount. Until recently you would have found the fifth Viscount ("Matt Ridley") in the opinion pages of *The Times* writing on environmental issues. If we'd have gone round the estate in the other direction we would have seen the open-cast mine on his land at Shotton. That's made him a controversial figure for other environmentalists who think coal should be banned as a fuel.

Things were much the same in Harper's era:

> Here the Ridleys have been seated for centuries, and from their wooded domain watched the belching smoke of the pits they own, which year by year have added to their wealth. Sir Matthew White Ridley, MP, is now the representative of these owners of mineral wealth and lord of Blagdon.

Quite pointed isn't he? It's one of Harper's little quirks that, while a staunch Conservative, he was never a big fan of the landed gentry.

Another claim to fame for the present lord involves a rather bizarre country park created by moving about 1½ million tonnes of rock, clay and soil a few hundred yards from

Shotton. Northumberlandia, opened just behind The Snowy Owl in 2012, has been landscaped into the shape of "a stylised reclining female figure clothed in grass". In other words it's a twenty-first century pit heap tarted up to pull in the tourists. "Lady of the North", boasts the sign outside. Sceptical locals prefer to call her "Slag Alice". It's free to enter, well-used by the public and seems to win awards, but to me it seems like the most basic kind of 3-D cartoon imposed on the land.

The previous evening I'd walked up to the summit – which happens to be Alice's face. The "sculpture" itself left me cold, but you do get fantastic views across to that rare thing in modern England – a working coal mine. Perhaps it was all those stories from Bentley, Ferryhill and Seaton Burn, but I was fascinated to watch miners at work – albeit miners above ground. Countless yellow dumper trucks scurry across a muddy landscape transporting their spoil like worker ants. At one end, hundreds of feet beneath a normal ground level, coal is being hewn and then transported up a steep but no doubt sturdy track. At the other end piles of the shiny black harvest lie ready to be taken away. The longer you watch the more mesmerising it becomes.

———

Dave and I get beyond the Blagdon Estate. A small, hump-backed bridge takes us over the River Blyth and then we start to climb, steadily but not uncomfortably. In this landscape, watercourses are everywhere, but they've got a new name. I associate burns with Scotland, but now there's a Duddo Burn to our left and a Catraw Burn to our right. Others called Pegwhistle, Cowclose and Whittle are in the same vicinity. Streams are just *so* yesterday. We then drift north east for the first of our Northumberland market towns. The approach to Morpeth is clean, green and immaculately tidy. We speed downhill, deep in a wooded cutting, pausing only to take a photo of a vintage cast-iron signpost which sums up the journey ahead. Alnwick is 20½ miles away, Berwick 50 and Edinburgh 110. Breaking news: Edinburgh has made it on to a signpost! The very fact makes me think that I might just do this...

The town centre itself is reached courtesy of a particularly fine bridge over our next river, the Wansbeck. Built in the 1830s, it replaced a narrower one which was demolished a few years later.

Harper detested that decision:

> No one benefited by its destruction, it stood in no one's way, and its utility was such that a footbridge, a graceless thing of iron and scantling, has been erected across those ancient piles, to continue the access still required at this point from one bank to the other.

For once I'm more interested in the newer model. It was built under the supervision of the engineer Thomas Telford and provides a glimpse of the Great North Road's most tantalising "what might have been" story. By 1820, stage coach travel ruled supreme. Yes, some sooty-faced visionaries were tinkering with steam engines in obscure North Eastern collieries, but at the time railways seemed little more than a cloud on the horizon. The great engineers were designing canals and roads – with Telford their undisputed master. Perhaps his finest work was the London to Holyhead road, including the magnificent suspension bridge across the Menai Straits. Much of this route is the current A5 and experts sing its praises to this day. Back then, the logical next step was a remodelling of the Great North Road and his surveyors spent eight years on the project. Telford's aim was clear: fewer bends, gentler hills and a shorter journey time. In his 1958 book *Thomas Telford*, the biographer L. T. C. Rolt quotes the engineer as he summarises the proposed route's specifications:

"A mail coach road of the most perfect construction and unqualified straight line from London by Barnet, Shefford, Newark, York, Newcastle, Morpeth, Wooler and Coldstream to Edinburgh may be reduced to 362½ miles; whereas the present hilly and incommodious road is at least 391½ miles."

Note that from Morpeth onwards, Telford was proposing an entirely different route – Wooler and Coldstream are much further inland. But by the time the plans were complete the climate had changed. The steam engine had puffed its way out of the coal pits and was well on its way to handling passenger traffic as well as freight. Roads were rapidly going out of fashion. And as a result Telford's reputation faded in comparison to the next generation of engineers – the likes of George Stephenson and Isambard Kingdom Brunel:

"Whereas the latter built their roads of iron, Telford laid his in water and in stone," wrote Rolt. "His achievement was as great as theirs and of equal historical significance, but his life's work ended just as the railway age began. Railways enabled a new industrial society to take another giant step forward and in the process Telford and his works were eclipsed: his roads fell silent and his canals slowly sank into neglect and decay."

In the end only the last 11 miles of the road into Edinburgh were built; or rather 11 miles of road and this new bridge at Morpeth. So in its own way the Telford Bridge is the last monument to the golden era of coach travel.

Immediately to the north of the river we find the Chantry Chapel, where our predecessors once had to pay a toll for crossing Harper's old, now-demolished bridge. Today it has two very different uses. Downstairs there's a conventional tourist information shop where the Geordie language is being marketed and monetised. Dialect words like "howay" – come on, "hinny" – a term of endearment, and "plodge" – to wade in the sea, are written onto hessian cushions which sell at £30 a pop. How do you say "You're having a laugh?" in Geordie, I want to ask.

But upstairs there's one of those quirky museums that seem to pop up in far-flung corners of the country. This one is dedicated to the history of bagpipes. Before you even get to the first floor your assumptions are firmly challenged by a notice on the wall.

"Most people think that all bagpipes are Scottish," it reads. "They are not."

Thus admonished, the visitor learns about Northumbrian Small Pipes, the last surviving kind of English bagpipe, an instrument where the air comes from a bellows rather than via a mouthpiece, resulting in a softer sound. They had once been popular right across the country, but lost out to the lute and the virginal in Tudor and Stuart times.

"Gradually," we're told, "the bagpipe became the instrument of the rabble."

I can't see this kind of museum ever getting the go-ahead now. Kids can't dress up, nor as much as touch a bagpipe, let alone try to get a tune out of one. But its sheer uniqueness means it really deserves a hefty grant – in perpetuity.

Morpeth's main street feels pleasantly old-fashioned. If locals want to pop to the shops, they park directly outside. Double yellow lines are minimal and those that do exist seem to be ignored. It's tempting to explore further, but there are about 50 more miles to be done, so after a quick coffee on Bridge Street, we turn right by the clock tower and head steeply out of town up Pottery Bank. Meanwhile the A1 does something momentous. After

290-odd miles of either two- or three-lane carriageway, it gets downgraded to one in each direction. It happens at the site of the old Loaning Gate Toll near the present-day junction with the A697 – Telford's chosen alternative route. Perhaps it's a secret monument by modern engineers to their founding father.

On our back road, that sense of being in Border Country grows stronger by the mile. After passing through the hamlet of Hebron, there's a sharp right-hander with spectacular views straight ahead of us. Hills are now everywhere, a wide variety of green and brown lumps and bumps in the foreground with darker, higher peaks lying behind, their summits invisible beneath low cloud. Next we spot a three-storey mini-castle amid a collection of farm buildings. Its size and its height make it look completely out of place in this sparsely populated landscape. Cockle Park Tower is a Peel tower, one of a number of fortified watch towers built on both sides of the border. Peel towers are a powerful reminder of an era when raiding parties could strike at any time, robbing people of their possessions and their livestock. Given enough notice, every local was gathered inside for protection.

The temptation, from the English perspective, is to talk about marauding Scots terrifying English settlements. The reality is that the so-called Border Reivers would rob and steal on both sides of the border, regardless of nationality. Lawlessness was the order of the day – complete with its own complicated set of family vendettas. The very word "bereaved" started life here. It meant to "be reived" – to have been attacked by the Reivers and to have lost property, livestock or kin. As a result, author and historian Dan Jackson memorably describes in his 2019 book *The Northumbrians* other parts of remote Northumberland as being "the Helmand Province of medieval England".

The key date in these parts is 1603, the year King James VI of Scotland became King James I of England. With a *united* kingdom to be consolidated, he was determined to hound the Reiver families out of existence. He succeeded, even if his methods were brutal. Large numbers of people were hanged – often without trial – and many more were banished to Ireland. The word "border" was itself banned; these lands were now to be called the Middle Shires. OK, the name didn't catch on, but it is true to say that a semblance of law and order was in place by the 1640s. So while fortified buildings might look unusual in most other parts of England, here they had become normal.

Cockle Park Tower was built in the early sixteenth century. The closer you get the more solid it looks. On two of the four corners, circular bartizans protrude in the manner of French castles while the sandstone walls are an incredible 1.5-metres thick. Harper says you can spot ten other Peel towers from its ramparts. It now forms part of an experimental farm run by Newcastle University – with visits strictly by appointment only.

———

We continue to plot a route north, with the A1 unseen to our west and the railway line to the east. Occasionally I call a time-out to scribble down some notes. As I'm busy, I'm slow to work out that Dave is now doing the same.

"Hang on Dave, I'm the one writing the book, what are you up to?"

"A poem."

"A poem?"

In all the years I've known him, Dave has never before given the impression that he might have a book of sonnets in his back pocket.

"Yeh, you're doing that daily thing on Facebook. I thought I'd do something different."

"So what have you got so far, then?"

"You'll see…"

———

Cycling is now a joy – poetry in motion perhaps. Overtaking cars are an occasional novelty, rather than a habitual nuisance. Settlements too, are few and far between. An unfurled Ordnance Survey map is able to make the point more eloquently than I can in words. North of Morpeth the map shows only three towns of any size at all. The first is Alnwick, our next destination; the other two are Amble on the coast with a population of around 6,000 and Rothbury with 2,000. That leaves around 1,000 square kilometres of field, forest and coastline.

We get back on the bikes. After a relatively flat interlude, we come across another gorge scoured deep into the landscape. The current A1 crosses the Coquet valley courtesy of a concrete viaduct slung across about 40 years ago. Until then every vehicle, however cumbersome, had to head steeply downhill toward the village of Felton along a road called The Peth. We do the same and, I admit, I come over all Welwyn. It's much smaller than the Hertfordshire village. But it is one of those little gems that catches me completely by surprise – mainly because both river and village are obscured by thick tree cover on the descent.

We cross the Coquet by means of a beautiful fifteenth-century bridge which Harper seems to have crashed his pushbike into. Although being Harper, the purple prose rather gets in the way of clarity:

> ... then precipitously down again through West Thirston and across the picturesque bridge that spans the lovely Coquet into Felton: villages bordering either bank of the river where the angler finds excellent sport, and where the rash cyclist, regardless of the danger-boards erected for his guidance on the hill-tops, tries involuntary conclusions with the aforesaid bridge at the bottom.

Involuntary conclusions? How much was the repair bill Charles, old boy?

Where I live in Norfolk, water moves slowly and silently through the landscape. Northumberland gradients add volume – in both senses. Today the Coquet chuckles contendedly underneath us, rippling around scattered stones upstream, dividing around a small island downstream. No doubt it also has uglier moods...

At the far end of the bridge a traditional red telephone kiosk has been reborn as The Info Box, complete with an array of tourist leaflets. Inside, a poster from the Felton and District History Society advertises a talk entitled "The Old Great North Road". I'm gutted to discover that we're out by five days, otherwise we might have quite fancied gate-crashing it, bikes first. Nearby, we get chatting to two gents who are tackling St Oswald's Way. This, we're told, stretches from Lindisfarne to Hadrian's Wall in honour of a seventh-century king of Northumbria. The older one doesn't tell me it's 97 miles long, he simply describes it as being "a canny walk, like". We're then asked about our route.

"I started at Newcastle, but Steve here's come from London," says Dave.

"Bad luck, someone has to," the younger one replies, quick as a flash.

On the south bank of the Coquet it is too early for an old coaching inn called The Northumberland Arms to be open, but on the other side we are sorely tempted by The Running Fox, a café with tables overlooking the river. If I had my time again I'd skip the Costa Coffee in Morpeth and hold on till here. The cakes are magnificent. North of Felton we zigzag across the A1, annoyingly racking up the gradients as well as the miles. Strange place names abound. In Swarland, Hazon and Guyzance, I feel as if I am in a different country. Traffic-wise it continues to be a different world too – noticeably quieter than anywhere in County Durham or North Yorkshire. In fact I think I'd have to go back to the stretch between Grantham and Newark for anything comparable. Dave's found a rhythm and is happy on the front bowling along without a care in the world. But hey, this is his Day One.

The approach to Alnwick is just as pleasant as Morpeth: more manicured lawns and sweeping descents. Top marks to the municipal gardeners of Northumberland, not a blade of grass has been out of place so far. Then we sweep past the quirky Barter Books, housed in a grand station building.

Is Barter Books the finest second-hand book shop in the land? In the world, even? It's certainly the most welcoming. Enter on a winter's day and you'll find a roaring fire in front of you with leather armchairs beckoning. A display directly next to the door seems designed to show off its owner's eclecticism. The last time I was there, it included books on bagpipe music, Native Americans, "The Geometry of Pasta" and shoplifting in eighteenth-century England.

It goes without saying that I love second-hand bookshops, but many have the same predictable flaws: higgledy-piggledy layout, monosyllabic staff and a smell of damp. Barter smashes those stereotypes – and others. It has lots of space, well-designed and well-signposted shelves in manageable sections and über-friendly employees. Most importantly, there are multiple places to sit and peruse – and it's warm, too warm even on occasion. All that's before you realise that there's a model steam loco making its way around a circular railway track above the top shelves for no apparent reason. I've come here for years. In the old days I used to think that all the customers looked like my parents. Now I've noticed they tend to look more like me, although to be fair there is a very decent – and occasionally raucous – children's section too.

But there are miles to be done, so on this occasion Dave and I speed straight past heading for Bondgate – a street with two names. The map shows that we're on Bondgate Without, which will soon become Bondgate Within. The reason becomes clear as we come up against Bondgate Tower, a three-storey lump of defensive stonework with a small archway pierced through the middle. Here it is. Border Country writ large in rough ashlar stone. The arch is only wide enough for one car – a serious impediment to modern traffic. Yet the main road between London and Edinburgh went straight through here until 1971. Top marks for history, bottom of the class for traffic flow.

We now very much feel *within*. Within the embrace of a proper Northumberland market town with a full range of shops alongside the cobbles.

A little way along, a shiny brass plaque outside The White Swan grabs my attention – and Dave is learning the hard way that I am physically incapable of cycling past any historical information board. A good job too, because this one is a cracker:

"Situated within this hotel is the first-class lounge from SS *Olympic* (1910–1936) twin ship to the legendary SS *Titanic*," it declares.

Dave holds the bike patiently while I head inside. And then a waitress waits patiently while I am allowed a quick gawp at the Olympic Suite. It is unbelievably grand: ornate wood carvings and panelling, sumptuous stained glass windows and an equally intricate ceiling and fireplace. It's very strange, not to say slightly eerie, to see an entire chunk of late Edwardian splendour designed for a luxury ship, now in dry dock at the rear of a pub in Northumberland.

Inevitably the plaque on the outside prompts a hundred questions on the contents within. I later discover that the *Olympic* and the *Titanic* were two-thirds of a family of three liners built by the Belfast shipyard Harland & Wolff for the White Star Line. Their varied "careers" reveal quite a lot about the early years of the twentieth century. The *Titanic* famously sank on its maiden voyage in 1912 after striking an iceberg in the Atlantic. More than 1,500 people died – largely because the boat was considered so unsinkable that there were only enough lifeboats for a third of those aboard. It exposed an incredible sense of hubris amongst the ship's top brass as well as the appalling class segregation that we remember from James Cameron's 1997 film. The *Britannic* was designed for the same market, but the timing of the First World War meant it was immediately requisitioned as a troop ship. It sank after hitting a mine in the Aegean Sea. Thankfully the designers had added more lifeboats after the *Titanic* disaster, so just 30 of the 1,000 passengers perished on that occasion. And then there's the *Olympic* – the great survivor. The *Olympic* also saw war service, but survived to undergo a luxury refit. It would become a favourite of royals and celebrities throughout the 1920s, finally being retired in 1935. Later that year it was brought to Jarrow on Tyneside to be broken up for scrap. And when the first class lounge was auctioned off, the owner of The White Swan was there with the highest bid. The hotel staircase and revolving doors at its entrance are from the same ship. In fact there are said to be hundreds of artefacts from the *Olympic* scattered across the North East. Apparently some of the poorest homes in Jarrow mysteriously acquired luxury carpets at this time – "liberated" from a ship which had finally gone out of fashion.

"Lunch," says Dave as those doors finally release me back onto Bondgate. "We need lunch, right now."

We do. We've covered 30 miles. We find the market place, complete with its octagonal market cross where royal proclamations have been read out for centuries. It's another timeless scene and I feel like I've gone straight from one film set to another. We lean the bikes against its lower steps and bag an outside table at Melvyn's Café. I realise I'm slipping into Northern ways, because we're soon chatting about the joys of Northumberland to a couple at the next table. But it doesn't take long:

"Where have you come from?"

"London, but…"

"Bad luck, someone has to."

Service at Melvyn's isn't the quickest, but when our all-day breakfasts eventually arrive they're enormous. We spend more than an hour sitting in the sunshine, refuelling and shooting the breeze. Eventually we head to the castle, catching sight of its battlements on our right at the same time as a larger-than-life-size bronze statue appears on the left. Striking a suitably martial pose, this is Alnwick's most famous son – Harry Hotspur. An arrow has landed at his feet and on each boot there's a star-shaped spur – although I can't help noticing how similar a knight's footwear looks to the cleated cycling shoes I'm sporting.

Born in 1364, Harry Hotspur won fame for his speed and prowess in battle. He was immortalised by Shakespeare and, later still, his name was used as the inspiration for the naming of Tottenham Hotspur football club. The reason? It's pretty tenuous, but in its early years, the team played on land once owned by his family, close to Tottenham Marshes. The real Hotspur was killed on the battlefield at Shrewsbury, fighting *against* Henry IV. So, despite many years of loyal service, he actually died a traitor. Luckily, having a really good nickname seems to trump all that.

Hotspur was a member of the Percy family and if you thought that 300 years of the Ridleys was impressive at Blagdon, it's nothing compared to their neighbours. The Percys have lived at Alnwick Castle for more than seven centuries, since 1309 in fact. But "lived at" isn't quite the right phrase. They built, defended, dominated and restored Alnwick Castle, fought battle after battle with the Scots and threw in the occasional rebellion against the English king too. Read any family history and you are likely to find phrases like "essential bulwark against the Scots". If they hadn't already existed, a London-based medieval monarch would have had to invent them.

We head along Narrowgate – predictably a bottleneck in the Great North Road days – until we reach our third film set of the day, the sturdy walls of the castle itself. Having not so much as glimpsed them from the town centre, their size and scale takes us by surprise. They must be more than 20 feet high. The barbican – effectively the entrance gate – is even taller and comes complete with slightly spooky life-size statues atop the crenellations. And then, before we really realise what we're doing, we're heading down another steep street – again called The Peth – toward the Lion Bridge over the River Aln.

The view is magnificent. The river in the foreground, the sloping grounds in the mid-distance and the castle dominating the ridge. Alnwick is the second-largest inhabited castle in the country and from here we can see its entire northern flank – a continuous line of substantial walls punctuated by towers – Constable Tower at one end, Abbot's Tower at the other. (Elsewhere, Avenger's Tower hints at dark deeds while Auditor's Tower feels almost ridiculously banal in comparison.) Within these outer defences lie the taller buildings of the keep itself, four storeys, glazed windows and a flag fluttering from a pole on the highest turret.

It's not a fairy-tale view as such, it's more rugged than that. But you can certainly see why it's featured in everything from *Downton Abbey* to the Harry Potter films – the castle now offers "broomstick training" in the Inner Bailey for an additional fee. Well, of course it does.

I take a photo of the Percy Lion on the bridge – he faces the Scots roaring defiantly – and realise that he's helped me make sense of the geography too. Of course you can't see the castle from the south. This was a building designed to defend the River Aln against invaders from the north.

We now, inexplicably, take a wrong turn. My only excuse is that I'm suffering from a peculiar form of bike indigestion – too much at one sitting after too long hunched over the handlebars. It's perfectly clear that the B6341 is the original GNR, taking travellers alongside the Heiferlaw (Peel) Tower before re-joining the modern road at Charlton Mires. But we manage to veer east to Denwick and then make a dog's dinner of the journey north. The only silver lining is this description from Harper of the route we missed:

> The road onwards is a weariness and an infliction to the cyclist, for it goes on in a heavy three miles continuous rise up to the summit of Heiferlaw Bank, whence there is a wide and windy view of uncomfortable looking moorlands to the north, with the craggy Cheviots, perhaps covered with snow, to the north west.

In my defence, our final destination for the day is on the coast – off the Great North Road but where the tourist accommodation is to be found. So we head north east, setting eyes on the North Sea at Craster. Here we head down to the tightest of harbours and watch a fishing boat being pulled out to sea with the help of what I can only describe as roller poles across the shingly foreshore. I taste salt in the air, I hear the gulls shriek above and I feel the low thud of the ice-cream van's diesel engine. The seaside in every sense, truly timeless.

We continue north through Embleton and Beadnell to Seahouses, from where three of the many Farne Islands are clearly discernible on the horizon.

We're booked into The Olde Ship, which we like from the moment we bump into the host in the beer shed outside. Inside, it's a Wednesday evening with all the attributes of a Friday night. At one end, a heaving bar with non-stop beery conversation; at the other, lots of holidaymakers tucking into fish and chips. I don't think I've ever been in a friendlier pub. Moreover, every inch of every wall is covered with nautical memorabilia: ship's lamps, a fishing basket, diving helmets, ropes, maps, life jackets, sou-westers and buoys. One chart, painstakingly hand-drawn, shows every Farne Island together with the position of each ship wrecked upon their shores. There must be 200 listed there.

I unfold my own map over a neighbouring bench. I always feel a bit self-conscious doing this in front of others, as if I'm an over-eager geography teacher on a Duke of Edinburgh trip. But, Dave, still cleaning up the last of his chips, seems to take it in his stride.

"It's alright till Berwick," I say. "But look at all this," I add, pointing to a rash of contours to the north. "This looks tricky."

"We'll be fine," he replies. "Anyway, I've got more important things to do."

We reach for our phones and settle into a companionable silence. I post my daily report online and get a few thumbs up from mates back home. Dave also presses send on what turns out to be a poetic epic, including such great lines as "Time for rest, more miles on the morrow/Some of Steve's shammy cream I might have to borrow."

I pretend not to notice that his "likes" soon double my own.

DAY TEN

SEAHOUSES TO DUNBAR

Day Ten

Seahouses to Dunbar

63 miles
2,875 ft of ascent

DUNBAR

✕
1650

Cockburnspath

Eyemouth

NORTH
SEA

Berwick-on-Tweed

Holy Island

A1
My route

Beal

Bamburgh

Belford

SEAHOUSES

N
NW   NE
W   E
SW   SE
S

As any cyclist will tell you, there's something strangely uplifting about being on the road early. Mostly it's a case of enjoying empty roads and morning light, but perhaps there's a smidgeon of smug self-righteousness too. MAMILs lying in? Never. As Dave and I wheel our bikes out of the beer shed just before 7.30 a.m., nothing seems to be moving in Seahouses, the only sound coming from the shrieking gulls. With a gentle westerly blowing in from our left, we pass the deserted crazy golf course, shout good morning to a couple of dog walkers and head along the coast road where camper vans have been parked up for the night, close to a lazy expanse of sand dunes. It's one of those wonderful May days when you know it's going to get warm, even if the thermometer can't confirm it yet. Gradient-wise it will be my toughest day but we're both up for the challenge.

On the horizon we can see our first objective: a smudge of grey on a stony outcrop which will later reveal itself to be Bamburgh Castle.

But as we get going my eye keeps being drawn across to the mysterious Farne Islands. Yesterday evening I'd spent a happy half hour hunched over a map working on today's route, but even then I found myself distracted by the jagged outline of rocks scattered across the North Sea. So scattered, in fact, that Knivestone, the most far-flung speck within the archipelago, lies well to the north of Bamburgh. Always a sucker for place names, I can't help but wonder who decreed there would be a Solan Rock and a promontory called Northern Hares. The maritime features sound more visceral. They include a bay called The Kettle and a host of channels called "guts". Churn Gut, Seal Gut and Scarcar Gut seem only to accentuate the danger to sailors – as witnessed by that long list of shipwrecks on the wall of The Olde Ship.

The most famous – if that's the word – is the *Forfarshire* which foundered upon the island of Big Harcar one stormy September night in 1838. When dawn broke, the plight of some of the survivors was spotted by Grace Darling, the daughter of the lighthouse keeper on the nearby island of Longstone. What happened next became the stuff of Victorian legend, arguably making the 22-year-old this country's first newspaper celebrity. Knowing that it would be impossible for the lifeboat to set out from Seahouses, she and her father William risked their lives by taking to a traditional Northumberland boat called a coble in an attempt to rescue the few survivors they could make out through their telescope. They rowed through Craford's Gut and around to Piper Gut where the *Forfarshire* had been torn in two. William leapt ashore to help gather the survivors, leaving Grace to hold the boat steady in the water. To their surprise there were actually eight men and one woman alive, together with the bodies of two children and one man. Now faced with an additional trip, William picked two crew members as well as two passengers for the first return journey. The extra muscle helped ensure that all were safely back at the lighthouse some two hours later. Against the odds, nine lives had been saved.

Clearly both father and daughter were heroes, but for the newspapers there was only one story. The plucky female, the windswept girl, the "maid of the isle". Grace Darling mania swept the country, prompting a demand for souvenirs and mementoes. People even wanted locks of her hair and fragments of her dress – which was carefully ripped up for the purpose. Photography had yet to be invented but insistent portrait artists were the equivalent of intrusive paparazzi. William Darling complained that they had been made to endure seven such sittings – a long and tedious process – in just 12 days. By the summer of 1839 hundreds of people were travelling to Northumberland and sailing for the Farne Islands in the hope of seeing either her or the site of "Grace's Deed" as it had become known.

Less well known is the fact that 43 of the 63 people on board the *Forfarshire* drowned that night. What's more, their deaths were arguably the fault of the ship's captain John Humble. He had set sail from Hull for Dundee at 6.30 p.m., soon after his vessel's boilers had been hastily fixed. When one sprang a leak midway through the voyage he could have headed for the nearest port. But he pressed on. The boilers failed completely, the winds became gale force and his ship hit the rocks at 4 a.m. The Grace Darling website – full of useful information on this subject – reports that a first inquest ruled the deaths had been due to "culpable negligence" on Humble's part. But the ship's owners and builders insisted on a second hearing which appears to have been more of a whitewash. This one decided that the deaths had been the result of "accidental drowning due to tempestuous weather".

As we get closer to Bamburgh I can start to pick out the pinkish tones in the stonework of the castle walls. Most photographers capture it from the north, putting the sea in their foreground. Perhaps that is the most picturesque angle, but on our road you get to see a true fortress looking down from on high. They're spoiled for choice with castles in Northumberland but this spot is surely amongst the most dramatic. It was built to guard a long since silted-up harbour within Budle Bay. To get there we have to turn inland. In fact from now until Edinburgh the east coast keeps turning widdershins (anti-clockwise). It's only to the north of the Firth of Forth that the British landmass expands eastwards again. To put it another way, if we were to head north from here we wouldn't make landfall until the other side of Aberdeen – more than 200 miles as the cyclist rides.

The castle is now upon us, even taller than I first realise. Perched atop a volcanic outcrop, it stretches across a quarter of a mile and eight acres, the most dramatic of settings.

A little further on there's the bonus of a spectacular cricket ground in its shadow. They've been playing here since 1895. The main road steers away from the headland as we pass the graveyard of St Aidan's Church where Grace Darling lies buried with much of her family. Directly opposite is the museum in her honour including the famous flat-bottomed and high-bowed coble used by father and daughter. It's much longer and heavier than I'd imagined – 300 kilograms-worth, according to the museum. A video recounting the rescue is played on the wall beyond the coble. Us visitors listen attentively, rather in the manner of an address at a funeral; the facts of the rescue told plainly and simply. Upstairs, they display some of the souvenir items from the time, their variety a testimony to the grip she had on the public's imagination: a snuff box, mugs, a paperweight and a china ornament depicting Grace straining at the oars.

———

We head west. Budle Bay is shaped like a mini East Anglian Wash, so we can soon see the coast again: mudflats punctuated by winding rivulets where hundreds of wading birds are on sentry duty. Inside my head, I'm aware of a new sense, not of mission accomplished, but at least of "mission under control". Setting off from London, I genuinely didn't know if I was going to make it. Now, I think I know that I will be OK. I've never run a marathon, but they say that the crowd helps you through the last few miles. Here, I feel the grandeur of the landscape is fulfilling the same role.

———————

Before long we're at Belford, back on the Great North Road. In the days of the mail coach, passengers enjoyed breakfast at The Blue Bell coaching inn – it was their second breakfast on the road if they'd travelled from London. Many complained that the service was too slow and the food too hot for the 15-minute break they were allowed. This is my tenth day out and I'm in less of a hurry. It's too early for a café, but the newsagent couldn't be more hospitable. Coffee comes from his Nescafé machine. Deckchairs are specially dug out of the back.

"There you go lads, lovely morning."

We now find ourselves sitting directly on my beloved road. Belford was bypassed in 1983 so it still looks like an original GNR village – particularly at this early hour when barely a car passes through. Two elderly locals shuffle in and out, each raising their furled-up newspaper by way of salutation and perhaps half an eyebrow at the cyclists lounging around, looking like they own the place.

Our route north takes us past The Blue Bell and then up a challengingly steep hill where I'm in danger of giving up. Dave, fitter than me and a football coach to boot, provides a stream of chirpy encouragement – the sort of thing I imagine he usually directs at his Under 14s. If I'd have got off once,

I'd have got off a dozen times. But reader trust me, our feet never leave the pedals. We pick up National Cycle Route 1 somewhere around Belford and the red-on-blue signs make our maps redundant. We're directed along helpful B-roads through hamlets like Detchant, Buckton and Fenwick where we come off the lower slopes of the Kyloe Hills and drop to the coastal plain next to the main road.

The A1 is again mercilessly unsuitable for bikes, so we take a side road toward Lindisfarne – better known of course as Holy Island, a centre of Christian pilgrimage for centuries. Cut off at high tide and reconnected at low, Holy Island is renowned for a sense of tranquillity and spirituality. Another diversion is very tempting, but the extra miles – not to mention the tidal complications – mean we head off-road along a bridle path instead. We soon end up on salt marsh where the only sounds come from a gentle swish of the waves and the odd rattle from my bike, complaining but coping on this rougher terrain. Dave – in contrast – is in his element, bouncing noiselessly along on his mountain bike, the front suspension taking everything in its stride. To our right we can now see both the island and a steady stream of traffic heading across the metalled causeway. I'd assumed this had been here forever; in fact it was only completed in 1954. Before then the only way was the Pilgrim's Way, a footpath across the mudflats marked by high wooden poles. This is how our St Oswald's Way friends would have started their walk – the ones we met at Felton. Today the wind is coming from the other direction, so not a sound comes across the water from either the causeway or The Snook – the strange, pan-handled isthmus of land that precedes the island proper. We might be some distance away, but across the gently shimmering sands, Lindisfarne still manages to maintain an air of mystery.

I head off into another daydream, this one prompted by a display at the local museum in Belford. It turns out that during the First World War this area of the coast was patrolled by a group of soldiers called the Northern Cyclists. The British Army was quite sophisticated at getting like-minded people to join up together. There were the famous Pals' Battalions of 1914 where people from the same factory or sports club would be encouraged to enlist en masse. Cyclists were targeted much earlier so that ten cycling battalions had been established across the country well before the First World War. The text from one recruitment poster ran:

ARE YOU FOND OF CYCLING?
IF SO
WHY NOT CYCLE
FOR THE KING
RECRUITS WANTED
BAD TEETH NO BAR

Why the last line? In the days before NHS dentists, dodgy teeth were commonplace – and sometimes proved an impediment to getting work. This phrase subsequently became famous, with old-timers successfully convincing more naive recruits that they wouldn't get served at the bar unless they sorted out their gnashers first.

The museum tells the story of Gateshead-born James Forrest who signed up upon the outbreak of the war and was stationed in the village from 1915. He fell in love with a shopkeeper's daughter and they married in 1916, shortly before he headed off to the front line. According to the museum, he joined the Machine Gun Corps and was killed just a few months later, one of 32 people from Belford who never returned. Going back a further hundred years, the display also includes an old coach ticket, the first I've seen. It entitled the owner to ride on the *Magnet* service between Edinburgh and Newcastle – but only on "the outsides", not warm and dry in the coach itself.

Our own northern patrol takes us to what looks like a classic Scottish links golf course – except that we're still in England. I pop into the Goswick clubhouse to fill my water bottle, quickly realising that we've left the Geordie accent behind. Everyone is up for a chat but the banter is more guttural and less melodic than I've heard for the last 100 miles. I'd have called it "Border", but according to the Northumbrian Language Society it's North Northumbrian. That's North Northumbrian as distinct from the Geordie accent of Tyneside and Pitmatic, the variant spoken in the former pit villages around Ashington. The accent, the coast and the vast empty acres all somehow create an impression that we're running out of England.

Harper tells us a good story about a post boy who was held up by a highwayman in this part of the world in 1685. That wasn't particularly unusual in itself, except that the highwayman was actually a woman, Grizel Cochrane.

> She waylaid the mail rider, and, holding a pistol to his head, robbed him of the warrant he was carrying for the execution of her father, Sir John Cochrane, taken in rebellion against James II... By this means she obtained a fortnight's respite, a delay which was used by his friends to secure his pardon.

A small copse of trees known as "Grizzy's Clump" had disappeared even by Harper's time, but her story survives by way of a Border Ballad. Of course there's a Border Ballad. As we continue this journey we will discover that every tale in these parts is celebrated in song.

Our path eventually upgrades itself to a tiny road with fantastic views toward what we assume is Scotland. Again there's not a soul to be seen, only the whoosh of an Edinburgh express train keeping us company on the main line. In the village of Spittal I spot my first orange and blue Irn-Bru sign above a shop, another indication that Scotland can't be far away. Spittal becomes Tweedmouth as we pass the lifeboat station and then we get the full vista of the Tweed. Berwick lies on its northern bank, looking as though it belongs to another country – which of course it did for spells throughout the Middle Ages. Below the red-tiled roof lines, every window looks out upon the river. Just like at Bamburgh, the brickwork has the faintest of pinkish hues. And protecting it all, sturdy ramparts close to the river's edge.

Sitting in my armchair back in Norfolk, Harper had annoyed the pedant in me when it came to Berwick. The Scottish border is more than two miles to the north of the town, so why did he describe it as being "geographically in the Northern Kingdom"? Fellow Great North Road author Norman Webster was even worse; he actually *starts* his Scottish chapter in Berwick. But overlooking the foreshore on Dock Road I'm inclined to eat my words. Yes, the current border has stood unchanged since 1482, but despite more than half a millennium of peace this still looks like a frontier. That river, those walls...

Before 1482 it had been a very different story. Berwick had been continuously fought over. The Scots would hold it for a while, then the English would retake it. In the previous 200 years it had changed hands on at least 13 occasions. That's bred an obdurate independence among its inhabitants which prevails to this day – they see themselves as Berwickers rather than either English or Scottish. My ear can't detect it, but apparently even the accent is distinct from its neighbours to the north and south. When I later ask around I get confirmation from the locals, although it's expressed with a shrug of the shoulders from people saying "it's a right old mix", rather than anything grander or more principled. The football team provides another anomaly. Berwick Rangers are the only English club to play in the Scottish League, allowing the author of one history of the club to title his book "An International Every Week".

————

It's southbound traffic only across the Old Bridge, so we walk across, savouring the significance of the moment. It used to be the border, after all. Built on the orders of King James VI of Scotland after he became King James I of England, it became an important symbol of his campaign to unify the two kingdoms. Perhaps there was a personal impetus too; James had been forced to cross a rather rickety wooden structure when he travelled south for his coronation in 1603. Today its 15 arches look low-tech compared to the more modern bridges upstream, but it still takes motor traffic.

Berwick is very much a town unto itself. Really it's worth a weekend all to itself too. Parts of it look like a smart Edinburgh suburb, elsewhere it has the feel of a provincial French town. It's still has a mile and a half of ramparts dating back to Elizabethan times. Stroll along them – it's virtually obligatory for visitors – and you really appreciate the scale of the Tudor project. This time the English weren't going to let it go. Substantial barracks remain too, these a legacy of the eighteenth-century Jacobite rebellions. The last soldiers left in 1963, replaced by a museum and rather less regimented staff. On the other side of the old parade ground you'll find the parish church, the only one in the country to be constructed during Oliver Cromwell's Commonwealth period. Built to his austere design principles with no tower or chancel, it looks surprisingly modern. All in all, history beckons around every corner. It's a struggle to drag ourselves away.

We climb steadily, passing the railway station and then getting a glimpse of the Tweed glistening in its valley to our left. We're forced to shadow the A1 – in bypass mode – for a few hundred yards until a tunnel sets us free, allowing us to head due north on the narrowest of lanes. To the right, Halidon Hill looks down on us. A battle here in 1333 saw the English beat the Scots. Until now the location of the battlefields I've passed can be at least partially attributed to their proximity to the Great North Road – generals normally like to march their soldiers along decent routes. But now it's all about the border. Halidon Hill, Homildon Hill, Otterburn, Flodden, Pinkie, Prestonpans and several other bloody conflicts can be blamed on that black line of dashes marking the boundary.

We carry on up our lane, wondering how much longer we can possibly remain in England. There are no signs so when we spot workmen renovating a building on the left-hand side of the lane, I take the opportunity to check.

"Excuse me, this might sound a stupid question, but are we in Scotland?"

"You are now."

"How do you mean?"

"That road's the border, the minute you stepped off it, you crossed the line. Welcome to Scotland."

"Err, cheers."

Confirmation comes when we cross the main road. To our right, a sign announces an entrance to Northumberland – "England's Border County". To our left, another proclaims that "Scotland Welcomes You". It's a big moment – even if the Scots make more of it than the English. It's no big deal, the English seem to be saying, just a new county. We decide to agree with the Scots and get the cameras out. Ten days after leaving the capital, I've crossed a national border. I do a rough, back-of-an-iPhone calculation and make it 420 miles of cycling. It would be an awful lot less as the crow flies or the car drives, but not half as much fun.

———

On the Great North Road itself, travellers used to cross the border at a building that was both toll house and marriage house. Of course the most famous destination for runaway couples looking to elope was Gretna Green, not least because the border on the west coast lies so much further south than it does on the east. But Scotland's more relaxed approach to wedding ceremonies meant there was a market at Lamberton Toll too. The building once boasted a sign saying "Ginger beer sold and marriages performed on the most reasonable terms" – which sums up the laissez-faire attitude very nicely. Coaches also did well out of the bridal trade. Often the same company would be hired by the escaping couple and the pursuing parents – without either side realising. Most of the traffic came to an end in 1856 with the passing of an act which required either bride or groom to have been resident in Scotland for at least three weeks. It's said that Lord Brougham, who steered the bill through Parliament, had himself eloped as a young man. During 37 years of unhappy marriage, he'd had plenty of time to regret his impetuosity.

By the 1970s the border on the A1 looked bleak. A modest Scotland sign stood next to the roofless remains of the toll house – since swept away. Now the dualled A1 offers a much grander entrance, with a long lay-by around a massive blue and white sign of welcome, just perfect for the selfie generation. Flags flutter from tall poles, though I can't help noticing that while those heading south into England get the red and yellow of Northumberland and a cross of St George, they also get a Union Jack. Heading north it's three saltires and that's your lot. You might also get a bite to eat at Adi's Diner. According to his board, Adi offers everything from Bad Boy Bacon to a Haggis Roll or an Egg and Tattie Scone although I must confess that I've yet to meet him.

The minute you cross the border, the A1 becomes more exciting and dramatic. To the left, the land tumbles down in a steep slope – with farm buildings on the summit – to meet the road, then green pasture split up by dry stone walls. Initially both road and railway line cling to a relatively narrow coastal ledge, full of a bright yellow gorse and the odd stunted tree, clinging on in the face of endless winds. Rail passengers, yet further down the slope, get the clearest view of the rocks below.

Harper, as ever, puts it well:

> Now the road runs upon the edge of black cliffs that plunge down into the North Sea, commanding bold views of a stern and iron-bound coast... Horses, coachmen, guards and passengers alike quailed before the storms that swept these exposed miles and even the highwaymen sought other and more sheltered spots.

In good weather it is no doubt a spectacular sight, though whenever I'm driving through it always seems to be "dreich" – the peculiarly onomatopoeic word for wet and dismal weather north of the border. But even through the sea fret, I love this stretch as a driver. Particularly where it remains a single lane in each direction, this is still recognisably the Great North Road of old. Only the soundtrack differs – the grind of powerful HGV diesel engines rather than the snort and spittle of horse power.

The road turns inland on the outskirts of Burnmouth, heading ever higher to the small settlements of Houndwood and Grantshouse, the latter being the point where the railway line reaches the summit of its 400-mile journey between London and Edinburgh. I feel for Grantshouse, there are clearly some well-loved houses and cottages there. But now we all speed through at 60 mph it's lost its raison d'être. A small petrol garage lies abandoned and several of the cottages look like they could use some TLC too.

———

Our route too has become more rugged. There's a relentless but scenic climb up to Lamberton Moor followed by a drop toward Ayton. The vista now couldn't be more vivid as we bowl through fields of oil-seed rape, their flowers poster-paint yellow, each one watched over by a noisy skylark. Looking across the valley of the Eye Water you can't miss Ayton Castle with its red sandstone turrets. You could call the architectural style "Disneyland fantasy"; the experts prefer "Scottish baronial". Either way the combination of a pink castle and the first *Daily Record* sign at the Ayton Mini Mart leave us in no doubt that we are north of the border.

Since Berwick we've swapped Cycle Route 1 for Cycle Route 76 and we quickly fall into the trap of following its signs rather than our own route. In his 2018 book *The*

Hidden Ways, the Scottish writer Alistair Moffat is much more dogged in his pursuit of the Great North Road in these parts. He establishes that the original route went straight through the castle's grounds. If Dave and I had indulged in merely the mildest of trespasses behind the castle's South Lodge, we would have found what Moffat describes as "a stubby little milestone, clearly old" with a faint "7" on one side, indicating the number of miles to Berwick. But those pesky bike route signs mean we're blithely adding extra miles by diverting to the fishing port of Eyemouth where the waitress at Mackays café laughs at our English accents and regales us with her dodgy Cockney impression. Welcome to Scotland. A cold wind never stops blowing at Eyemouth; it's only from within the warm windows of the café that I can appreciate what a tight little harbour it is, the waves crashing in upon the Hurkur Rocks.

After Eyemouth the only way is up, but we've found our climbing legs now and encourage each other onwards. Dave does particularly sterling work on a ruler-straight section across Coldingham Moor. We're running parallel to the A1, a few miles to the north, but this A1107 seems to have been a recognised alternative in the old days. And despite the A-road status, there's little in the way of traffic. At the top we are rewarded with fantastic views of the coast. The map shows a jagged shoreline of dramatic cliffs and small beaches, but all we can see are arable fields, sloping down to the bluest sea I've ever witnessed in the UK.

Somewhere in that panorama is Siccar Point – an almost mythical spot for geologists. It was here, in 1788, that James Hutton and colleague John Playfair found evidence of two different rock formations right next to each other. The fact that one was horizontal and the other vertical, helped prove that natural forces had shaped the world over many millennia rather than the much shorter Biblical timescale. According to the Scottish Geology website, Playfair later recalled that "the mind seemed to grow giddy by looking so far back into the abyss of time."

Less weighty matters concern us because we're now heading downhill. Not heading, but hurtling in fact – every stretch through gorse-lined hedges, nothing short of exhilarating.

"I've picked the best bit of your trip, haven't I," shouts Dave as he overtakes me, both of us hitting speeds of 35 mph plus. It's hard to disagree, harder still to catch him up.

We were expecting Pease Bay to be a bona fide village, in fact it's simply a holiday park – sleepy at this time of year. The bikes deal with their first ford of the journey – a gentle splash across Pease Burn shortly before it meets the sea. Now basking in warm sunshine, we climb back to the A1 past Cockburnspath where Route 76 takes us across a tougher river, a ravine in fact. Dunglass Dean has presented a challenge to engineers for centuries, but now five bridges of various vintages cross within a few hundred feet of each other. Our one dates from 1797 – the second oldest, but most elegant. Stopping for a photo, I put the bike in front of its crenellated parapets. The arch of the railway viaduct is directly behind, with the straight lines of the A1 road bridge a little further beyond. In between the two, a tiny semi-circle frames the sky meeting a hazy North Sea.

From now until our destination in Dunbar the contours are kinder. We race north along the old Great North Road before joining a bike path alongside the current A1. Torness Nuclear Power Station – painted pale blue in a vain attempt to blend in with the skyline – pops up on the coast before we escape onto a side lane. Our road then becomes a path in the lee of the railway line, but thankfully some freshly laid tarmac keeps us motoring. We only realise how recent it is when we see the guys from A. G. Thomson & Sons laying the latest steaming stretch in front of our very eyes. Thanks fellas.

Keen to crack on, we pay little attention to the village of Broxburn on our right and the distant peak of Doon Hill to the left. But this was the scene of another of those Border battles that seem to litter the landscape hereabouts. The Battle of Dunbar took place on 3 September 1650 and forms part of the Third Civil War when Oliver Cromwell was fighting the Scottish. He was retreating from Edinburgh with a weakened army in the face of a determined push by the Scots under their general Sir David Leslie. Cromwell was in danger of being encircled at Dunbar, indeed an ignominious retreat by sea may have been his only option – his own Dunkirk, as it were. Leslie's men approached Dunbar from the south and held the dominant position along Doon Hill, but the general was persuaded to come down to the lower ground by officers impatient for a quick win. Cromwell saw them on the move while walking with his staff in the gardens of Broxburn and instantly recognised the opportunity. Leslie's men were now wedged between the higher ground and the Brox Burn. Dave and I cross this, barely noticing there's even a bridge, but further west it is – or least was – deeper and more of a morass.

In his 2006 book *Cromwell's Masterstroke*, military historian Peter Reese explores the build up to the battle. "The Lord hath delivered them into our hands," Cromwell is said to have declared. "They are coming down to us."

His troops attacked early the next morning and delivered as resounding a victory as Edward III had at Halidon Hill three centuries before.

"With a force so reduced in number and ravaged by illness, the daring of the decision to strike at any enemy almost twice their strength needs no emphasis," writes Reese in his examination of the clash. "In no other battle since 1644 had a commander knowingly accepted such adverse odds for what Cromwell accepted would be his 'masterpiece or his misfortune'".

These days suburban Dunbar reaches out almost as far as Broxburn. Harper describes it as being "the first characteristically Scottish place to which we come". That feels spot-on even if I can't quite explain why – yet. I leave Dave at the hotel and head to the museum housed within the Dunbar Town House.

Dunbar was a royal burgh, one of about a hundred towns granted certain privileges over the years by a succession of Scottish kings. The three essential components of a royal burgh were a tolbooth, a kirk and a mercat cross. That's a tolbooth rather than a tollbooth. This side of the border they lose an "l" and gain a considerable amount of grandeur. The tolbooth at Dunbar, complete with its semi-hexagonal stair tower and tall spire, is considered a classic of its type. While the buildings were originally designed to collect tolls, they later became the Scottish equivalent of a town hall – complete with everything from a small jail to a council chamber. The example here is said to be the oldest functioning chamber in all of Scotland. As for the kirk, I'd passed it on my way down – a red sandstone church with high gothic windows overlooking the sea. Its tower is presumably as much of a landmark to passing ships as it is to those of us on terra firma. And after a bit of confusion I realise that I'd walked straight past the mercat cross outside the town house. Mercat is simply the Scots word for market. The cross signified the right for traders to meet and sell, but in Scotland it seems to have a higher profile than in England – the one we leaned our bikes against in Alnwick for example. In Scotland the cross is the acknowledged centre of the town – a place for proclamation and celebration.

I wander down to Victoria Harbour. On my bit of coast in Norfolk this would have been prettified and gentrified, but here it still feels like a place of work. The battered remains of Dunbar Castle are at its far end guarding a narrow entrance. The bricks of the surviving walls – and the colony of kittiwakes – seem to blend in with the natural rock and it's only one lonely fragment of a tower that really tells of its antiquity. Perhaps the most famous story here goes back to the fourteenth century when Black Agnes, the Countess of Dunbar successfully withstood a siege from a vastly superior English force while her husband was fighting elsewhere. Named for the colour of her hair, she not only rebuffed the Earl of Salisbury's men, but seems to have positively revelled in it. After the English battered the castle walls, she sent her maids out in their Sunday best to ostentatiously wipe away the marks with their handkerchiefs. Salisbury's huge battering ram was itself battered by large boulders dropped from the ramparts and an attempt to have her brother hanged in front of the castle was treated with contempt. Agnes simply pointed out that if he was killed, she would inherit his earldom. History, it seems, is everywhere more vivid here – as much legends and heroes as bloodshed and battle.

I grab an impromptu seat on a pile of yellow crates left unattended by the fishermen. Looking out towards the mouth of the harbour, I contemplate just one more day in the saddle. If you'd have asked me at Grantham or Northallerton, I'd have been happy simply to limp into Edinburgh. Now all that's changed – I feel I could keep going to Inverness if I had to. Is that my body adapting, my mind accepting, the weather improving or the wind shifting? Perhaps cycling with company helps. Or the increasingly spectacular scenery. It's hard to say, and probably unwise to analyse. Just savour the moment. Once again tonight's place of rest is very different to last night's – the joy of the open road. The fact that we've crossed a border today makes it all the more obvious. I simply resolve to appreciate all the tiny differences – everything from accents and attitudes to banknotes and beer.

———

Later in the evening I walk back into town with Dave. After a full-on day, we need refuelling. We decide against the Black Agnes restaurant in favour of Ristorante Umberto. We are both – how can I express it – satisfyingly knackered. I may have done more miles in a day back home, but I've never climbed this much. Every muscle in both legs aches, but the left thigh is worse than anywhere else. Could that be because the pannier is on the left-hand side? Would it work like that?

Food-wise, we've chosen well. Umberto's is a throwback, a quality old-fashioned Italian.

"It's my wife's birthday tonight," Dave tells the waiter. "I should be with her, but look at us."

Dave calls Lindsay back home and jokes about his romantic meal while I tuck in. After ten days I finally nail the perfect evening meal for a hungry cyclist – a pint of Belhaven Best followed by an awful lot of spaghetti carbonara. Why has it taken me so long?

DUNBAR TO EDINBURGH

Day Eleven

Dunbar to Edinburgh

35 miles
925 ft of ascent

FIRTH OF FORTH

Bass Rock

DUNBAR

EDINBURGH

East Linton

Longniddry

Prestonpans

Traprain Law

Haddington

Musselburgh

✕
1745

	A1
	My route

N

NW NE

W E

SW SE

S

I sleep well. We both sleep seriously well. It's the deep sleep of cyclists who put in a decent shift yesterday. OK, 62.8 miles including 2,875 feet of ascent to be precise. I start to accept that I am demob-happy. I dare to think that today should be a doddle in comparison and I finally realise that I'm missing my family. But first, breakfast. At 8 a.m. the Dunmuir Hotel is packed with a surprisingly cosmopolitan mix of tourists and business people. Surprising, until I realise that after a few days off the beaten track, we're starting to feel the centrifugal forces of a capital city down the road. I choose Scottish porridge cooked to order – simply because I've crossed the border and it would feel rude not to. We also notice that haggis has joined black pudding on the breakfast menu – which is now called a Full Scottish.

We cycle back into town. When we reach the end of the high street, we do something momentous – we turn left. To be fair, heading in any other direction would put us in the sea, but more importantly Dunbar is the furthest point north on my journey. The remaining miles will see us head west – with a hint of south – across a mixture of craggy coastline and the rich, agricultural land of East Lothian. If Thomas Telford had got his way, the improved Great North Road would have avoided all this. His route would have ploughed directly across the Lammermuir Hills to approach Edinburgh on the diagonal from Morpeth – shorter by distance but higher by gradient. Looking at the map you can't fail to notice how ambitious those plans were. Apart from a narrow coastal strip, I see a chart thickly striated with orange contours around a variety of "dods", "laws" and "heughs". As we've heard, the coming of the railway meant Telford's road never got built. All these years later the modern A1 remains pragmatic, hugging the coast as far as Dunbar before turning inland.

Harper talks of leaving the town via "wriggly and exiguous streets, coming through the fisher villages of Belhaven and West Barns". Well, if those streets are still there, we don't find them. In fact we head out along the most scenic of coast roads seeing no evidence of commercial fishing, but increasing signs of an economy tilted to tourism. Beautiful Belhaven Bay is known for its surfing while the wider area is marketed as "The Golf Coast". We pass our first links almost immediately. In all there are 21 courses in this part of the world, including Muirfield – the famous Open Championship venue.

Out to sea, we get a view of Bass Rock, a volcanic lump of an island which guards the entrance to the Firth of Forth. It's only later that I discover that the lighter streaks of colour come from the sheer number of gannets on its cliffs. Or, in truth, gannets and their guano. Bird and rock are so interlinked that the Latin name for the species is *Morus bassanus*.

In the foreground, we look out to the John Muir Country Park, named after a native of Dunbar who made a name for himself in the United States. In his early adult life Muir was something of a wanderer, a solitary journeyman who found work and friends where he could, but enjoyed the solitude of America's great outdoors when he couldn't. After nearly losing his sight in 1867 he resolved to explore for exploration's sake, reawakening a love for nature first kindled on this stretch of coast. He's remembered now as one of the fathers of the conservation movement in the United States. Incredible as it sounds, President Theodore Roosevelt was persuaded to turn Yosemite into a national park after going on a camping expedition with Muir in 1903.

"I do not want anyone with me but you, and I want to drop politics absolutely for four days and just be out in the open with you," he told Muir.

A photo at the museum shows the two of them looking across the high mountains, Roosevelt with a kerchief tied around his neck, Muir with his trademark straggly beard stretching halfway down his chest. It's hard to see that sort of excursion happening with a twenty-first century president. Soon after the trip Roosevelt introduced legislation to set up five national parks and many more national forests. Muir's place in history was assured, but more importantly the idea of the national park became lodged in the American psyche. More than a century later, many an American comes to Dunbar on pilgrimage having completed the John Muir Trail in the Sierra Nevada mountains. They visit his museum and then set off on the coast to coast John Muir Way – Dunbar to Helensburgh.

For a few miles at least, we follow the same route. Then both Bass Rock and the country park disappear as we strike out inland along the original Great North Road as it falls into the valley of the Scottish Tyne. Does today feel different? Is it because I'm travelling west, after ten days of due north? Once again my mind races away – simply because I'm on a bike. For five minutes I allow myself to think that I am rediscovering the finely tuned internal compass of our nomadic ancestors, before reminding myself that I'm actually a 50-something office worker on a fortnight's jolly with a map in the pannier and tracking software on the phone.

We're back on Cycle Route 76, but in this neck of the woods that means a pavement directly alongside the A199 – safe but dull. East Linton provides a bit of interest with a noble old bridge across the Tyne – solid sixteenth-century brickwork in pinkish sandstone. It's my second Tyne of course and another of those places where I'm tempted by the idea of an impromptu diversion – perhaps heading upstream to the river's source in the hills south of Edinburgh. There's no footpath as such, but the sign on the gate suggests there doesn't need to be. This is Scotland, where the law gives everyone a right to roam across land and water as long as they behave responsibly.

Harper liked this spot. After crawling through the meadows, he writes, the Tyne "plunges here in cascades under the road bridge, amid confused rocks". I'm starting to realise that the further away from London we get, the less likely things are to have changed since his day. And that realisation brings forth another: the further away from London we are, the more I can trust his descriptions. Whenever I re-read a passage about a place after cycling through it for the first time, I invariably find myself not only agreeing with Harper, but wishing I could express my own thoughts so vividly.

"What kept you?" asks Dave as I finally scramble up to the road.

"My Victorian hero and some pioneering Scottish legislation," is what I don't reply.

After East Linton we should rejoin the A199 but we're happily led astray by Route 76, climbing steeply to the south of the Tyne Valley along the beautiful and beautifully named Brae Heads Loan. Roads are smaller in this landscape. Even the A1 seems tiny. It swoops across our road by way of a sinuous concrete bridge perched on surprisingly slender legs either side of the river. Beyond, a volcanic hill looks down on us. This is Traprain Law, a place which has seen human habitation for thousands of years. A hoard of Roman treasure was found here in 1919. The discovery was fresh in

Harper's mind when he published the second edition of his book in 1922.

"At first the 'finds' were of minor articles: bronze ornaments, glass and pottery, fragments of iron, mostly of Celtic origin, but some Roman," he wrote. "The great discovery was made on May 12th, 1919, when a workman, driving a pick through the floor, brought up a silver bowl on the point of it."

They'd discovered a deep recess filled with treasure, 250 items weighing over 22 kilograms – the largest collection of Roman silver ever found outside the empire. A lot of it had been cut up. In Harper's era it was thought that such destruction was the work of barbarian tribes with no appreciation of the quality of the items. But the latest theory is that in troubled times, silver had become bullion – which is why each cut item weighed roughly the same. So rather than plunder from raids, this treasure may well have been a bribe from the Romans further south to persuade a native chief not to launch attacks in their direction.

History continues to come thick and fast. Within the shadow of Traprain Law we find Hailes Castle, abandoned and ruined, but with memories of Mary Queen of Scots as well as Great North Road favourites Harry Hotspur and Oliver Cromwell. The famous son of Alnwick tried to take the place twice, but was fought off on both occasions. The information board can't resist a football allusion – Hailes 2 Hotspur 0 is the headline. Cromwell was more successful. His forces largely dismantled the castle during his 1650 campaign. So England won the replay… is what the board doesn't go on to say. Dave, I discover, doesn't do castles. He guards the entrance while I traipse across every blade of grass, running up the wooden staircases like a seven-year-old to see how the walls stand sheer above the Tyne. I do love a crenellation.

Dry stone walls now replace hedges as our road tumbles down into Haddington, a town with a relatively small population but a grander past. "Comfortable and ample" is how one 1950s gazetteer described it. We turn right at the old starch mills, pass the tiny Golf Tavern and approach the river next to Georgian-style houses painted inviting shades of cream and ochre. Crossing by way of a twelfth-century bridge, we see a very different Tyne from East Linton. Here, it's placid, providing a perfect reflection of the whitewashed pub on one bank and a church that looks more like a cathedral on the other. St Mary's, it turns out, is the longest parish church in Scotland. They call it "Lucerna Laudoniae" – the lamp of the Lothians. Alongside the churchyard look out for St Mary's Pleasance – a recently restored walled garden. Designed by a former director at Kew Gardens, it includes a laburnum walk, a cottage garden and an orchard full of fruit and nut trees. The man from Kew wanted to fill it with traditional varieties – a Cosford Cob hazelnut and the Merryweather damson for example.

The town centre is just around the corner. It feels like Dunbar – four-storey houses, a little austere to English eyes, but well-kept and brightly painted in a variety of soft pastels. True, there's a Tesco elsewhere but on the high street the chain stores have yet to make a mark. All in all, Haddington feels like a small cathedral city – a learned library here, a "purveyor of fine cheese" there. It's also the "capital" of East Lothian with a row of smart, municipal buildings along Court Street to prove it. I would call it the "county town" but that expression doesn't seem to really work north of the border.

The A199 continues to plough west. This stretch goes down in Great North Road folklore for being the scene of a violent protest against the London to Edinburgh mail coach just a few weeks after it was established in 1786. Stage coach owners across the country resented the introduction of the new service. And here they bribed a number of local carters (effectively the HGV drivers of their day) to block the road as the coach approached.

According to the *Caledonian Mercury* newspaper from 21 December 1786, the guard – armed and encouraged by his passengers – told them to clear the way, as was his right. They, in turn, laughed in his face. A fight followed, with both guard and coachman given a thorough beating. I love the level of detail in these old reports. As the journalist puts it: "Too much praise cannot be given to the guard who, twice beat down with the instrument of death in his hand, never offered to level it at his adversary."

In that era an "s" was often written as an "f". In the *Mercury* article, the report states that "a fcuffle enfued...

involving a blundebufs." In that form and at this distance it appears faintly comical but these *gilets jaunes*-style demonstrators were subsequently given jail sentences for their trouble. In retrospect they got off lightly; impeding His Majesty's mails would later become punishable by transportation or even death.

Sticking to the Great North Road means putting up with another pavement, so we're happy to escape north along the route of an old railway line. After more than 400 miles, I've long since lost the fear that *there won't be a way through* on two wheels. It's now crystal clear that throughout the UK there will always be a bike-friendly alternative as long as you're not too fussy about your precise route. Without traffic to worry about, Dave can monitor our speed in real time. Laden down as we are, we easily average 18 mph along this flat track. The only thing to hinder us is a plethora of historical and botanical information boards which even I am happy to ignore. On either side we pass rich, arable fields with earth as pink as any Devon soil. Old writers talk of this part of Scotland as being the "fabulously rich red lands"; certainly our bikes are caked in a fine, red dust by the time we reach Longniddry.

———

Meanwhile the Great North Road continues through Macmerry and Tranent. They were places of industry in the

Harper era – iron founding and coal mining in the main. As such, he gives them short shrift. He found Macmerry to be "an ugly row of cottages on either side, with cinders and dust, clinkers and mud... and some gaunt works within eyeshot". Those single-storey cottages are still there, smart slate roofs and double-glazing now of course, while the works have all gone, replaced by first an RAF airfield and latterly an industrial estate. Harper is even sniffier about Tranent which gets described as "a townlet subsisting upon collieries: how grimly commonplace!" It wasn't alone, this stretch of Lothian was home to substantial coal mines with thousands of men working a 7-foot-thick deposit known as the Great Seam. They'd been digging here since the early thirteenth century. Even by 1547 the underground shafts were substantial enough to hide all of Tranent's inhabitants when English soldiers came through – the English too could maraud when it suited them. The last deep coal mine closed in the 1960s, but an open-cast one continued until 2000.

Our old branch line deposits us at Longniddry station, from where we hurry down to the sea alongside the walls of a country estate. We last saw this coast at Dunbar, but the Firth of Forth has narrowed dramatically in the meantime. Now, what all the books seem to call "the ancient kingdom of Fife", is more visible on the other side. It's easy to make out the twin peaks of East and West Lomond, but otherwise the land appears cloaked in a velvety navy – quite alluring in its own way.

We stop, take stock and stare out to sea. In the estuary itself, Bass Rock has disappeared, replaced with another island – Inchkeith. While Bass Rock was used as a place of political exile – "Scotland's Alcatraz" according to the local paper – Inchkeith was used for medical quarantine. In the late fifteenth century they included people with syphilis, in the sixteenth century it was the plague. Elsewhere, you can find at least a dozen "Islands of the Forth" with names to tickle the imagination – Fidra, Inchmickery, Craigleith and the Isle of May. Their histories are varied but there are common themes. First, ancient saints with associated religious buildings; later, castles and forts squabbled over by Scottish, English and French forces and finally a more peaceful present as nature reserves. Two have also attracted high-profile owners. Inchkeith is run by the founder of the Kwik Fit chain, another called The Lamb was bought by the famous spoon-bender Uri Geller.

"The asking price was seventy-five thousand pounds, but after negotiations we were able to settle on a fee of just thirty-thousand," Geller says on his own website.

Then Edinburgh appears on the horizon. Well, not the city as such, but the outcrop known as Arthur's Seat, just to the east. We're more than ten miles away, so it feels suitably ephemeral and ethereal at this range – my final destination, marked out by an extinct volcano named for its connections with the legendary king. I take an ostentatiously deep breath. I can feel a sense of quiet satisfaction seeping through my body. I say it again, I am no kind of natural sportsman – just a bloke who likes cycling, had a goal and did a bit of training.

On the road, there's yet another golf course to our left and Longniddry Bents to our right. My Scottish vocabulary widens again – bents are a place where reeds or rushes grow. Half marsh, half dunes, I guess. Dozens of birds chirrup in the trees and dog walkers emerge at unpredictable angles. By Port Seton we're directly back on the coast looking across at an expanse of teeth-like rocks and salty pools. But the line of sight keeps changing. Arthur's Seat has gone again and it's more difficult to work out where our side of the Firth of Forth begins and ends. Straight ahead, part of Fife gets erased behind a rain shower. To our right, a solitary ship heads eastwards.

It's now a very decent day to be by the seaside. A large holiday complex gives us the impression that we're approaching bucket and spade land, but the villages of Cockenzie, Port Seton and Prestonpans resist such descriptions. Throughout the centuries this part of the coast has worked hard for its living. Indeed, much of Tranent's coal left the area through these harbours. The colliery owners had built wooden waggonways as early as 1722 – taking inspiration from those in North East England. Some of the black stuff was used to produce salt by heating seawater in massive pans, hence the whitewashed salt workers' cottages off Cockenzie high street and the very name Prestonpans.

Salt production continued day and night, the fires providing a landmark for ships at sea. Only on a Sunday would they be allowed to go out. Coal was also hewn on the coast itself. And when the Preston Links colliery closed it was replaced by the Cockenzie Power Station – the largest of its kind in the country. Its giant chimneys were demolished as recently as 2015, but the coal store is still there, so too the branch line and giant electricity pylons.

So, to us at least, these villages don't feel like resorts. There's a walkway along the coast, but you'd struggle to call it a promenade. Fishing feels more important than tourism. We stop briefly at the harbour where a fisherman is hard at work behind the lobster pots. Closer inspection reveals he's battling with a crossword rather than his nets, but hey, we all need a break. All in all, Scotland is steadfastly refusing to be twee.

Perhaps inevitably this part of the world was also the scene of yet another battle – the last I'm going to mention on this journey. The Battle of Prestonpans is actually the favourite of all my Great North Road scraps, not least because the underdogs pulled off an unlikely victory – the might of the British state beaten by Jacobite rebels. The former should have thoroughly defeated the latter, but, on 21 September 1745, the Redcoats under Sir John Cope turned and ran in the face of a Highland charge. It prompted much soul-searching from the Hanoverian government, although Cope and his two deputies were later cleared of any wrongdoing. Ultimately the tables would be turned the following year at Culloden, so this victory heralded only the briefest of honeymoons.

I'd previously read up on how the armies had got here. Cope's forces had marched from Dunbar, the rebels from Edinburgh, led by Bonnie Prince Charlie.

"Bonnie he was not," says author Martin Margulies in his 2007 book *Battle of Prestonpans*. "Alcoholic, narcissistic, paranoid and a spouse and partner abuser, he was a pleasant enough fellow when he got what he wanted, but so are most people."

Cope and his men camped in a field which offered a good defensive position, facing his enemy to the west and protected by a marsh to his east. But overnight the rebels used a secret path through the marshy ground to surprise him in the early morning gloom. Within a matter of minutes this initial offensive had completely spooked the Redcoats, who ran for their lives and, in many cases, toward their death. So complete was the rout, adds Margulies, that on the losing side "none of the soldiers attempted to load their pieces again and not one bayonet was stained with blood".

Like any good battle, it's spawned a few myths. First, that Cope slept soundly in a comfortable bed at Cockenzie, completely unaware of his enemies' movements; second that in the headlong retreat, he was that rare creature, a general who brought news of his own defeat to the wider world. According to Margulies, neither are true, but they're certainly good enough stories to weave into a Border Ballad taunting Cope. The chorus runs:

> *Hey Johnnie Cope, are you wauking yet?*
> *Or are your drums a-beating yet?*
> *If ye were wauking I wad wait*
> *To gang to the coals i' the morning.*

Wauking, it should be said, translates as waking.

At the end of Cockenzie high street Dave and I find ourselves at the house where Cope's war chest was inexpertly hidden before it was confiscated by the victors. All of these battle locations are more cheek-by-jowl than I'd realised. That, and the sudden discovery of a special Prestonpans 1745 app, means we're again tempted into a diversion. A few clicks later and the GPS-enabled guide has us heading toward the route of an old waggonway. I'm now used to the idea of battles being contested across the Great North Road, but it's a surprise to find one being fought on a very early railway line. Halfway along a dusty path, we find two symbolic tombstones raised off the ground: one in red sandstone to the memory of the Jacobite soldiers; another in yellow limestone for the government soldiers.

Guided by the app's walking tour feature, we then follow the trail to a tall, pyramid-shaped viewing platform. It's a struggle to push the bikes up the steep slope, but the view is worth it, even leaving aside the battle. The whole of the

Firth of Forth now lies in front of us with the pattern of settlement very clear. Towns and villages gather on the coastal strip, hemmed in by the railway line to Edinburgh. Around us, a greener belt; although giant yellow digger trucks lumber across a neighbouring hillside.

"All that," says a dog walker at the summit, "used to be an open-cast coal mine. But now they're building thousands of homes. All this," – and now he gestures to the rolling fields – "is prime agricultural land. They're completely changing the nature of East Lothian."

It's something I've been noticing without acknowledging since Dunbar. On the outskirts of every town and village, new housing estates are going up. Edinburgh's commuter belt is rolling eastwards at quite a pace. Standing on this bing (the Scottish word for a pit heap) we are witnessing a landscape in transition. I take another look at the information panels. There's an atmospheric illustration of the Highlanders moving three abreast in the dark along the secret footpath. Alongside, a decent explanation of what went so wrong for the Hanoverians:

"A bayonet could be fitted onto the musket, but a redcoat was not equipped for protracted hand-to-hand combat. The British Army was trained to fight regular European armies. These men had never faced a Highland Charge."

We speed down one of the four edges of the bing to a gorse-fringed path next to the railway line. There's time for one more memorial – an obelisk in honour of Colonel

James Gardiner, one of the few government soldiers to fight with any honour. Then we swing under the railway bridge, through Prestonpans town centre and back to the coast. This is where the old Great North Road finally gets close to the sea, approaching Musselburgh via its famous racecourse. But we're car-free, riding in on a mixture of rough asphalt and smooth tarmac at the water's edge. Sea then becomes tree-lined river – cycling along the banks of the Esk really is the only way to arrive. Musselburgh bustles on the high street and luxuriates on the riverbank. It's got a prestigious boarding school, a relatively new university, three golf courses and a tolbooth with the trademark tower. It's noticeably more prosperous than its neighbours to the east.

We have a choice of seven bridges across the Esk, but for us it has to be the five stone arches of the New Bridge – the one that took A1 traffic until 1987. Once across the river, we are in the suburb of Fisherrow – once famous for its fishwives, a close-knit group who would not only clean, gut and prepare the fish their husbands had caught, but would also carry them into Edinburgh to be sold from massive wicker baskets. With distinctive striped skirts and aprons, they were a familiar sight until well into the twentieth century. Throughout their history they were seen as being unusually independent, not telling their husbands how much they earned, for example. According to the John Gray archives back at Haddington, they held an annual Shrove

Tuesday football match – married fishwives versus the unmarried, if that isn't a contradiction in terms. A sense of fierce identity and independence means they are now hailed as early feminist heroes.

We continue along the A199 and are welcomed to Edinburgh by a large purple sign, belatedly realising that the tiny Brunstane Burn beneath us must be the border.

A more obvious boundary arrives when we escape onto a beachside walk as Joppa becomes Portobello. Those single-storey buildings at Cockenzie have long-since given way to three and four-floor Victorian villas. There's even a retro-Citröen called The Little Green Van selling flat whites to well-dressed millennials. On Portobello high street there are two artisan bakeries and a blindingly white bookshop full of titles I fear I am not cool enough to read. In the front window of a gift shop an old poster shows the Art Deco lines of the Portobello Open Air Pool. Long demolished, it once counted a young Sean Connery among the lifeguards.

We have lunch at an upmarket café directly on the promenade before belatedly remembering that we're meant to be following the Great North Road. We head inland blindly, but pick up the Fishwives Causeway – entirely by good fortune. If it was good enough for their wicker creels of fish, it's good enough for us. We eventually rejoin the A1 close to Jock's Lodge – which always gets a mention in the old books, despite the fact that no one knows anything about either Jock or his dwelling-place. In Harper's time it was:

... a district slowly emerging from the reproach of a disreputable past, when footpads and murderers haunted the muddy roads, or took refuge amid the towering rocks of Arthur's Seat ... or the congenial sloughs of the Hunter's Bog.

Today the area seems to be better known as Willowbrae – just another Edinburgh junction, where purple buses tangle with cyclists in the bus lane. As I ride I realise that a separate part of my brain is telling me that *I'm almost there.* My mind races back through the highs and the lows until my daydreaming affects the quality of my riding, resulting in an impatient hoot from a bus driver. *One pedal stroke at a time,* I tell myself – particularly as we're back in the sort of traffic I haven't seen since the Holloway Road.

A new Meadowbank stadium is being noisily constructed on the site of an older version. Buses and fast food joints multiply. We start to climb. We get the occasional view of Arthur's Seat as it pops out between new-build flats. As the buildings get more elegant, we take a left fork, looked down upon by storey upon storey of sash windows. Our road gets steeper and leafier, but there's no question of us dropping the speed let alone the gears. Even if the holiday coaches weren't giving the game away, the topography is slowly revealing Edinburgh in its three-dimensional glory. We pass the many monuments of Calton Hill – the first indication that this is a capital city, not just any old metropolis.

Then, quite suddenly, a view opens up. To our left, the Salisbury Crags end of Arthur's Seat, below us, the railway lines snaking into Waverley Station. Beyond, the famous old town: buildings of every height and design; sooty sandstone and shiny glass; spires and cupolas – layer upon layer of both architecture and history. Half of me wants to race on to the finishing line, the other half, simply to stop and stare. It's the kind of view that you probably don't get time to appreciate if you arrive by car. This is one of the many advantages of cycling – the chance to pause wherever you want, freed from the tyranny of parking restrictions.

Regent Road gets grander, its buildings taller and more civic in function. Still obsessed with my Great North Road mission, I can't quite work out whether the A1 ends at the junction with North Bridge or once the same thoroughfare becomes Princes Street. But for our ceremonial purposes it ends at the Scott Memorial amid the chatter of thousands of international tourists. Dave congratulates me with a solemn handshake, but I'm actually a little lost for words. I've done nothing else for the past 11 days but concentrate on getting from capital to capital. What I was going to do when I got here has been completely beyond me.

For some reason I want to head straight to the station, but Dave wisely advises a trip to the Old Town first. We've got to see something of Edinburgh before we leave. So we cross North Bridge and head up the beautifully curving Cockburn Street – surely the most characterful in the city. The details of its smart Scots baronial style pass us by, but the circular window rooms beneath conical towers certainly give the shops an air of sophistication. On The Royal Mile, the crowds thicken and the tartan teddies proliferate. We walk up as far as St Giles Cathedral in Parliament Square. Nearby a squat stone monument looking like an oversized pulpit piques my interest. It takes a while for me to realise that this is Edinburgh's Mercat Cross – considerably grander than the one in Dunbar and with a unicorn on top of the column where I would have expected to see something cruciform. Important proclamations, I learn, are still made from this very spot. That, I decide, can finally be that. My journey ends here in the very heart of my second capital city with 493.4 miles on the clock. I retreat to a shop, buy a handful of postcards and return to the cross.

Alongside the address, I write just two words on each one: "Made It!"

AFTERWARDS

Edinburgh Waverley is packed with rugby supporters arriving for a big game. Fans mingle happily but noisily. Their chants bounce off the walls, drowning out more traditional station sounds. We weave our way through the replica kits and get the bikes stowed in the goods van. Even sitting down in a carriage feels indulgent.

Within two hours of arriving in this city I am already leaving. Once we pull out of the station I can't take my eyes off the windows as all that territory I've won is thrown into high-speed reverse – back along the coast to Longniddry and then fast across the fields to Dunbar. Disappointingly, a North Sea *haar* – a spring and summer coastal fog – obscures what would have been spectacular views along the cliffs to Berwick. We change trains at Newcastle and take a commuter service to Cramlington – really only just down the road from The Snowy Owl. The bikes now go on the roof of Dave's car before we hit the A1. More memories engulf me. The Angel of the North, Darlington, Wetherby, a dodgy crossing at Foston, my mini-meltdown at Grantham. Eleven days of hard graft now summed up in just a few hours – like watching a highlights film.

By 1 a.m. on the Saturday we're both back at our homes in rural Norfolk. But on Sunday morning at the usual time, Dave and I are back at the war memorial to meet up with Jim and Nige. Dave F., Sean and Lindsay are there too – the full weekend crew.

It's time for another ride.

CHARLES G. HARPER

1863–1943

Harper was nothing if not prolific in word and well-travelled in deed around the turn of the last century. He covered more than 2,500 miles on foot and by bicycle to research the 13 major coaching roads of Britain across 15 years and 17 volumes. But even during this period of his life, he was publishing other titles with extraordinary regularity. Away from topography there were two volumes of *Stage Coach and Mail in Days of Yore* as well as *Highwaymen of England* and a novel called *Hearts do not Break*.

Charles George Harper was born at Bayswater in London in 1863. He has no biographer as such; much of the detail I include here comes courtesy of an eight-page article published in the *Antiquarian Book Monthly Review* in 1975. Fellow author Norman Webster – who had just published his own book on the GNR – came to know him in the latter years of his life and was keen to commit his memories to paper.

After boarding school in London, Harper became a printer before starting to submit articles to magazines where, as Webster puts it, "he could express himself freely in his topographical causeries". He would very quickly get the hang of it. Always an illustrator, his first book, published in 1892, is called *English Pen Artists of Today*. But within a year he had also produced *The Brighton Road, Old Times and New on a Classic Highway*. He wrote this as a personal journey, a style he would continue for *Paddington to Penzance* published the following year. Here his second day begins as follows:

"This morning there was an indignant man to breakfast at Cookham. Nothing pleased the creature and the crowded coffee room was well advised of his discontent."

For his later books he would be happy to let the road be his narrative thread. Now the only person who could be indignant would be Harper himself as this "stalwart Conservative" indulged in occasional sallies against either the Liberal or the Labour Party. His one blemish at this time is an 1894 polemic called *Revolted Women*. It's an angry diatribe against any member of the female sex not placidly remaining in the home. The language, of course, seems outrageous to modern eyes, but I'm not convinced it wasn't seen as rude, wrong and over the top even by the standards of his own time.

The series on England's coaching roads, widely seen as his classics, was completed by 1907. He then turned his attention to the south coast, producing volumes to cover the coastlines of Cornwall, Devon, Somerset, Dorset and Kent. Next he switched to literary and legendary figures for *The Hardy Country, Summer Days in Shakespeare Land* and *The Ingoldsby Country*. After the war he was snapped up by publishers wanting up-to-date travel guides for motorists. But leafing through gazetteers like the *Burrows RAC Guides* and the *Newnes Motorists' Touring Guide*, you can feel him going through the motions, producing, in effect, "Greatest Hits" summaries rather than anything fresh.

Webster is keen to stress how private Harper was as a person. Shortly after his death, he visited his home in Petersham, near Richmond in Surrey:

"Harper, so eloquent in expressing himself on the English countryside, was curiously guarded in revealing details of his personal life," he wrote. "Such facts as I could muster came from his secretary and from the silent testimony of the notes and papers on his desk."

He died on 7 December 1943.

So we must rely on his books – an anecdote here, an autobiographical snippet there. In the *Newnes* guide, he features in a photograph, but his face is obscured by the windscreen while his (female) chauffeur smiles for the camera. I like to think that this meant he had softened in the 30 years since *Revolted Women*. He would surely have railed against the very existence of a "chauffeuse" in 1894.

Today his books are rare and getting rarer. But his illustrations have recently been given a new lease of life by Historic England, the public body given the job of protecting the country's historic environment. The organisation more typically deals with archive photographs, but within the last few years it has catalogued more than 1,100 of his original drawings. Together they provide, it says, "an artist's impression of a 'Lost England', showing idyllic scenes of towns and villages before the large scale development after the Second World War."

Much as his words continue to do today.

TOP TEN TIPS FOR BIKE TOURING

Tip 1 – Look after your backside
Skimp on proper cycling kit if you have to, but get the best pair of padded shorts that money can buy. And by the same token, get some decent chamois cream. Don't wait until there's a problem, get it in the pannier.

Tip 2 – Eat properly
I got this one wrong too, suffering that mini-meltdown on Day Four because I was running on empty. If you're on a bike you will burn plenty of calories. Eventually my food formula settled down to include a Full English breakfast first thing and plenty of pasta with a pint in the evening. Get some flapjack in the pannier for emergencies, but keep it away from the shammy cream.

Tip 3 – Midweek training
Train over consecutive days if you're going to cycle on consecutive days. Too many of us just do the "weekend warrior" thing.

Tip 4 – Enjoy yourself
Take photos and keep a diary. Your journey is going to be great, but you'll forget so much of the detail unless you record it at the time.

Tip 5 – Explore
And on a similar note don't be a slave to The Route. If the road less travelled looks more interesting, take a punt. You're unlikely to be back this way again.

Tip 6 – Get up in the morning
Early miles are good miles. Get on the road by 8 a.m. and the day will fall into place. And of course there will be fewer cars too.

Tip 7 – Back up
If you're recording the miles on an app, bring a spare smartphone. My first one died in a Cambridgeshire motel and it took a while to get a replacement forwarded on.

Tip 8 – Free cancellation
Keep your hotel/Airbnb bookings as flexible as you can. There will be days when 60 miles are a breeze, others where 35 feel impossible.

Tip 9 – Get good tyres
Punctures bad, Schwalbe Marathon Plus good.

Tip 10 – Communicate
Talk to people. You're on a touring bike, you're on a journey. People expect you to have a story to tell. Don't disappoint.

THE GREAT NORTH ROAD COACHING INN

In the old days, passengers leaving London on the Edinburgh mail might well have stayed at The Saracen's Head on a street called Snow Hill before they started their journey. Sadly, the inn is long gone. These days Amazon's sleek London HQ looks down on one side while some rather sad-looking former Smithfield Market buildings survive on the other. But look closely and you'll find a former police station tucked in there too. Between the Sherlock Holmes-era police lanterns, a plaque proclaims it to be "SITE OF THE SARACEN'S HEAD INN, DEMOLISHED 1868".

Charles Dickens knew it. Of course he did. He chose a coffee room next to the inn's booking office as the place to introduce us to Wackford Squeers, the cruel head teacher of Dotheboys Hall in *Nicholas Nickleby*. It must have had a wider frontage then, stretching up to that rare survivor from the old days – St Sepulchre's Church on Holborn Viaduct. Certainly it was big enough to handle more than 30 coaches a day, many of them heading north. We know what the accommodation looked like, because Charles Harper included an 1855 illustration within the first volume of his *The Great North Road*. It shows three storeys of galleried landings around a central courtyard – strangely not dissimilar to the balconies of 1960s American motels. Now, London's only galleried inn is to be found south of the river. The George at Southwark is such a curiosity that it's owned by the National Trust but leased to Greene King. Thankfully you can still get a drink after all these years.

So where might I find the perfect surviving coaching inn? Such a thing probably didn't exist 200 years ago let alone now, but that didn't stop me searching.

The Wellington at Welwyn was the only one worthy of note across the first two days. Dating back to 1352, it counts both of Britain's favourite Samuels among its distinguished guests. Dr Samuel Johnson was a regular while Samuel Pepys, writing in 1660, was full of praise:

"And so rode to Welling where we supped well, and had two beds... And still remember it that of all the nights that ever I slept in my life I never did pass a night with more epicurism of sleep."

Airy and spacious, its owners did a super job in bringing it up to date after a fire in 2009. Relatively recent restorations are a common theme. You could argue that it's only in the last 30 years or so that we've really started to appreciate their importance.

On Day Three, classic inns suddenly came thick and fast. **The Bell at Stilton** looks gorgeous, inside and out. Just a casual look from the pavement would guarantee it a top ten spot: a beautiful limestone facade combined with an impressively weighty pub sign. Inside you get to lap up the history surrounding its famous cheese too.

The Haycock at Wansford is less than ten miles further north. Grander, but less homely than The Bell, it looks magnificent – particularly from the outside. Remove the cars, add a four-in-hand and the years would simply fall away.

Yet **The George at Stamford** trumps both of them. Once again it dates back centuries, its gallows sign daring to cross the Great North Road itself. Stamford manages to be both timeless and busy. So while The Bell and The Haycock seem happy to rest on their laurels in somnolent villages, The George still gets to bustle. And remember those separate facilities for people travelling north and south: the London Room and the York Bar. Wonderful.

This far from the capital, coaching inns start to have a different feel. They dominate their high streets – with space for substantial stabling and kitchens. Both had to be large enough and efficient enough to stick to the strict timetable demanded by the mail coaches. There was also the buzz created by being at the hub of the most up-to-date form of communication. These were places at the very centre of their social and political worlds.

Heading north, both Grantham and Newark disappointed, leaving **The Bell at Barnby Moor** to fly the flag for the East Midlands. The interior of The Bell is effortlessly refined. Nothing has been updated needlessly, yet everything works perfectly. If we were to drop a resurrected Harper into the building it would take him a while to realise that he'd landed in the wrong era. No one does wood panelling better. And the leaded windows are to die for.

Moving into Yorkshire, I wanted to like **The Crown at Bawtry** not least because it's the only inn which still declares itself to be a Posting House. But inside, the inn fails to reflect its history. For me this is a modernisation that hits slightly the wrong note.

I'm sure both Doncaster and Tadcaster had great inns at one point, but I failed to find any survivors. So thank goodness for the **Sant' Angelo at Wetherby** which offered fine dining and a decent atmosphere on a Saturday evening.

In North Yorkshire both **The Crown at Boroughbridge** and **The Golden Lion at Northallerton** were outstanding. They're proper inns, not just pubs. Pubs provide food and drink, inns offer accommodation too. The welcome needs to be warmer – and in my experience it always is.

North of Northallerton I really struggled. In Northumberland **The Blue Bell at Belford** might once have had a certain something, while Dave and I managed to draw a complete blank north of the border – although I am sure The George at Haddington would have been atmospheric if only they hadn't converted the building into flats and painted it pastel shades of sky blue and cream.

So where is the perfect coaching inn? I was probably looking for some sort of amalgam of the holy trinity at Stamford, Barnby Moor and Northallerton until I found out about The Three Tuns at Scotch Corner. The Three Tuns no longer exists but for a while it looked as if it was going to be recreated within the grounds of Beamish Museum in County Durham.

Beamish is a special place – a vast open-air site sat within 350 acres of rolling farmland. Modern life disappears once you cross the threshold, replaced by a variety of buildings from a variety of eras. Visitors happily stroll away from a 1900s pit village to immerse themselves in the world of Pockerley Old Hall – the home of a well-to-do tenant farmer from the 1820s. Until recently a big expansion of this Georgian section was to include the complete reincarnation of a coaching inn – complete with accommodation to allow people to stay the night.

Back in 2019 I sat down with one senior member of staff who enthused about how guests would be given food, drink, even entertainment from the time. They'd draw the line at bed bugs and straw mattresses, but pretty much everything else would have been authentic.

"I've got this idea that I'll retire, come down to The Three Tuns, sit here in the corner wearing a smock, drinking beer, smoking an old clay pipe and telling people that it used to be all fields round here once," he told me.

Then the coronavirus pandemic struck. The paying public had to stay away and budgets were drastically recalculated. Visiting the location of the inn in late 2020, I found only wooden hoardings around a building site. This exciting project is at best delayed and at worst stalled indefinitely. But it's such an innovative idea that I remain positive that it will be resurrected – one day.

Really my journey ended in Edinburgh. But I want it to end with a pint in the tap room of a Great North Road coaching inn in exile.

Here's to the very idea of The Three Tuns. May it be built at some point. And may it be a warm and friendly memorial to a grand old road.

ACKNOWLEDGEMENTS

Thanks to my wife Debbie and our daughters Abbie and Maya for putting up with constant diversions off the A1 to look for Great North Road memorabilia that was of no interest to them whatsoever.

Thanks to sister Caroline for happily ploughing through the archives from Kew as well as a myriad of archived newspapers. Thanks to Caroline and Mum for their patient proof-reading and Dad for his expertise on railway and engineering matters. Thanks to a brace of brothers-in-law – Colin Bagust and Dave Rowland – for their *directeur sportif* duties across Nottinghamshire and Yorkshire. And to Dave and sister-in-law Sue for putting me up in Lincolnshire.

Thanks to the many members of the Loddon Mountain Bike Club (Minus the Mountains) for helping to get me in good enough shape for The Big Ride. Jim Stuart also provided a morale-boosting motorbike escort across Day Two while Dave Matthews was my lead out man for the last three days. Dave, that unsigned copy is yours.

Thank you to everyone I met along the route – the camaraderie of the road is a wonderful thing. And to the many hotel staff who were kind enough to make sure my bike was looked after and locked up in function suites, boiler rooms and beer sheds. Sorry about all the mud.

Finally a massive thank you to everyone at Summersdale for turning a spare bedroom project into a living, breathing book. I must particularly thank Debbie Chapman for her unfailing positivity and expertise at every stage, Ross Dickinson for his laser-like focus on improving my writing and making me answer unanswered questions and Neil Kelly for assiduously fact-checking and copy-editing my script.

ABOUT THE AUTHOR

Steve Silk is a journalist working for BBC Look East in Norwich.

The Great North Road is his third book, after *The Wherryman's Way* and *Hidden Riverside Norwich* saw him explore the Norfolk Broads on foot and by canoe. *The Wherryman's Way* won the East Anglian Travel Book of the Year award in 2010.

Steve lives in Loddon, Norfolk with his wife Debbie and their two daughters. You can follow him on Twitter @Greatnorthroad2.

He is now looking closely at the A40 – the old London to Milford Haven road taking in the Chilterns, Oxford, the Cotswolds, Gloucester and parts of the Brecon Beacons. Once again he would be following in the tyre tracks of Charles Harper. Once again he might need a new bike.

SELECT BIBLIOGRAPHY

General first – then from south to north

Charles G. Harper – *The Great North Road: London to York,* 1901

Charles G. Harper – *The Great North Road: York to Edinburgh,* 1901

Norman Webster – *The Great North Road,* 1974

Frank Goddard – *The Great North Road,* 2004

Chris Cooper – *The Great North Road Then and Now,* 2013

F. H. West – *The Great North Road in Nottinghamshire,* 1955

Roger Protz – *Historic Coaching Inns of the Great North Road,* 2017

Norman Webster – "The English Traveller: Charles G. Harper, 1863–1943", *Antiquarian Book Monthly Review,* issue 16, 1975

Leslie Gardiner – *Stage Coach to John O'Groats*, 1961

W. Outram Tristram – *Coaching Days and Coaching Ways*, 1893

Sir William Addison – *The Old Roads of England*, 1980

Brian Paul Hindle – *Roads, Tracks and their Interpretation*, 1993

Geoffrey Hindley – *A History of Roads*, 1971

F. E. Baines – *On the Track of the Mail Coach*, 1895

David Smurthwaite – *Battlefields of Britain*, 1984

L. T. C. Rolt – *Thomas Telford*, 1958

Andrew Emmerson and Peter Bancroft – *A, B, C and M: Road Numbering Revealed*, 2016

R. C. and J. M. Anderson – *Quicksilver: A Hundred Years of Coaching 1750–1850*, 1973

Daniel Paterson – *A New and Accurate Description of all Direct and Principle Cross Roads of England and Wales*, 1808

Frederick Wilkinson – *Royal Mail Coaches: An Illustrated History*, 2007

S. H. Moxham – *Fifty Years of Road Riding: A History of the North Road Cycling Club*, 1935

Dorothy L. Sayers – *Lord Peter Views the Body*, 1928

Tony Rook – *A History of Hertfordshire*, 1997

Steve Cooney – *Images of Tempsford*, 2007

Ned Boulting – *On the Road Bike*, 2013

Trevor Hickman – *The Bell, Stilton* (leaflet)

David Clark – *Battlefield Walks: The Midlands*, 1993

Rupert Matthews – *The Battle of Losecoat Field*, 2013

William Stukeley – *Sir Isaac Newton's Life*, 1752

Margaret Thatcher – *The Autobiography*, 2013

John Speed – *Theatre of the Empire of Great Britain*, 1606

Nicola Davison-Reed – *Retford Through Time*, 2012

Nicola Barber – *Who Journeyed on the Mayflower?*, 2014

Rodney Cousins – *Newark Inns and Public Houses*, 1991

Tom Bradley – *The Old Coaching Days in Yorkshire*, 1889

John Evelyn – *The Diary of John Evelyn: Vol. 1*, 1818

Robert Unwin – *Wetherby*, 1986

William Camden – *Britannia*, 1607 edition

Alfred Wainwright – *A Coast to Coast Walk*, 1973

Samuel Tuke Richardson – *Family Annals by Road and Rail By Flood and Field*, c.1890

Richard Evans – *The Essential Guide to Beamish*, 2017

Ian Nairn – *Nairn's Towns*, 1967

Dan Jackson – *The Northumbrians*, 2019

Gemma Hall – *Bradt Slow Travel: Northumberland*, 2019

Ian Hall – *Highways and Byways of Northumberland: The Great North Road*, 2015

Eleanor George – *A Walk Around Felton*, 2013

Belford and District Local History Society – *Belford Village Trail*, 2015

Alistair Moffat – *The Hidden Ways*, 2018

Keith Fergus – *Lothian and Berwickshire Coast*, 2013

Peter Reese – *Cromwell's Masterstroke*, 2006

Martin Margulies – *The Battle of Prestonpans*, 2007

Websites:
SABRE – sabre-roads.org.uk
Boroughbridge Town Council – www.boroughbridge.org.uk
Durham Mining Museum – dmm.org.uk
Grace Darling – www.gracedarling.co.uk
Uri Geller – www.urigeller.com
Evening Chronicle – www.chroniclelive.co.uk
Scottish Geology – www.scottishgeology.com

INDEX

INDEX

INDEX

Have you enjoyed this book?
If so, why not write a review on your favourite website?

If you're interested in finding out more about
our books, find us on Facebook at **Summersdale
Publishers,** on Twitter at **@Summersdale** and
on Instagram at **@summersdalebooks.**

Thanks very much for buying this Summersdale book.

www.summersdale.com